£8.50

Michael Fordham once described himself as 'the only Jungian in the world interested in children'. He has always been a controversial as well as a key figure.

In this thoughtful memoir he remembers his childhood in Surrey and Hampshire, his early training as a doctor and his work in a mental hospital. He writes candidly about his battles against the tendency to religiosity and cult formation within the Jungian fold and outside it; and in supporting the study of the self in childhood, a phase of development he felt Jungians neglected to their cost. There are also memorable portraits of Jung himself, of the Jungian communities in the United States, of the evolution of British psychotherapy and child guidance; and of the revelatory impact of the mother–infant observation work of the Tavistock Clinic, London, which he encountered late in life.

MICHAEL FORDHAM, a leading figure in the Society of Analytical Psychology and Honorary Fellow of the British Psychological Society, was a founder member of the Royal College of Psychiatrists. He was the first editor of the *Journal of Analytical Psychology* and co-editor of C.G. Jung's *Collected Works*.

Michael Fordham

Photo: James Astor

THE MAKING OF AN ANALYST

A MEMOIR

MICHAEL FORDHAM

'an association in which the free development of each is the condition of the free development of all'

Free Association Books / London / 1993

Published in Great Britain in 1993 by
Free Association Books Ltd,
26 Freegrove Road,
London N7 9RQ

ISBN 1-85343-305-5

The frontispiece and illustrations on pp. 8, 10, 14, 19, 43 and 76
are reproduced by kind permission of Michael Fordham, his family
and James Astor. The photographs of C. C. Jung and Emma Jung
on pp. 68, 78 and 114 are reproduced by kind permission
of the Familien-Archiv Jung.

A CIP catalogue record for this book is available
from the British Library

Printed in the EC by The Cromwell Press

CONTENTS

Preface   vi

1   The Fordhams   1
2   The Worthingtons   7
3   My Parents   15
4   Limpsfield, 1909–1918   24
5   Removals   27
6   Hillcroft   30
7   Hampstead and Catastrophe   38
8   Cambridge   46
9   St Bartholomew's Hospital   52
10   Psychiatry, Child Guidance, Analysis   59
11   Transition: Nottingham, Wartime   81
12   London and Analytical Psychology   91
13   Editing   103
14   Jung   111
15   Journey to the United States   121
16   The Society of Analytical Psychology   127
17   Ageing   139

Index   146

PREFACE

I have called this book *The Making of an Analyst* because I hold
that there was more than training, more than making a career and
earning a living in it. Nor in my case was it only a matter of choice,
for there was an inevitability about it and the eventual recognition
that no other occupation suited me. Words like vocation, or phrases
like 'way of life' occur and seem more or less appropriate but
unsatisfying – they are tarnished yet they are near to what I mean.
Another way of looking at it is to say it involves a commitment to
self-realization – a life-long quest, and I think that was a powerful
motif at one time. Like others, I thought that this aim was vitally
important not only for oneself but also for humanity, in as much as
we were contributing to a new science, which Jung especially had
initiated. This would provide the means whereby mankind could
develop a new consciousness so that the periodic catastrophes
which man instigated could be transformed into creative achievement.

All that comes into it, but if I look back on my life – as I do in this
book – it seems different. I could say that my theory of the self in
childhood originated at the breast, reflected in the omnipotent
fantasy of being in the centre of the world of railway trains when
sitting on my mother's knee at Clapham Junction, or that then I had
the first intimation that the self was important, as something greater
than me, yet of whom I am a part. If I look through my life from that
vertex I come to striking conclusions. The failures that I describe
here all seem to prevent me going in the wrong direction: failure in
the entrance examination for the Navy; failure to do well enough
in the Cambridge tripos to engage in research; failure in the MB
examination which prevented me becoming a house physician on
the Unit at St Bartholomew's Hospital; running out of money so that
I could not become a neurologist – all these events pushed me in
the right direction. But it was not until my analysis with Godwin
Baynes, however disastrous others may have thought it, and my
meeting with Jung, that I knew what I wanted to be – a Jungian
analyst, in which all my talents could be combined and I could arrive
at maximal self-realization through individuation. I arrived there by
a mixture of chance and good luck but I have a strong sense that

the pattern of my life was predetermined, however much I disbelieve in such exaggerated propositions as hocus-pocus.

Jung once told me that when young he thought that human beings were peculiar and incomprehensible, which was a reason for his trying to find out about them. I cannot say that I arrived at that conclusion until I started to be an analyst, but I have come to be amazed at them and myself; it still seems to me astounding that I have had quite considerable effects on analytical psychology, not only in stimulating interest in childhood but also in promoting Jung's discoveries, clarifying the method of analysis and describing what goes on between analytical psychotherapists and their patients. I still think it astonishing that at the age of eighty-eight I continue to analyse and teach and that human beings will ask me to continue to do so. For many years I could not tolerate praise but at last I have come to recognize that it is often genuine and that I have been a man who has done good in the world.

There have been events in my life of which I am ashamed or even horrified, but these have been mostly secret, though I have tried to indicate them and so give a more rounded picture. A friend of mine remarked that an autobiography is a sort of lie about oneself – I recognize what he meant, but I have tried to be as truthful as I am able. Indeed, this essay started from a purely subjective position: I wrote it first for myself with the idea that I might have a small number of copies made and circulate them amongst friends and others whom I thought might be interested. Consequently it began by containing 'reminiscences' in the sense that it was composed of memories as they came to mind. I made no attempt to ascertain whether they were historically correct: they were memories as they occurred in my mind as I wrote them down – in that sense only could they be treated as factual. My idea was that these 'facts' represented those which were active now and were, or rather still are, influencing my mental and emotional life; they are indicators of my personality.

Though broadly there is a historical perspective in it all, I have not kept to that all the way through. I am aware that there is something 'childlike' in the language of the chapters on my childhood, while later chapters are more controlled by their subject-matter: for instance, those on Jung, analytical psychology and so on; subject-matter that occupied me over many years. As the writing developed, I showed my product to friends and relatives, meeting with surprising appreciation and suggestions that I should go on and publish the result. When I had got further on, I submitted the result to Free Association Books, who accepted it and offered to provide editorial assistance by Karl Figlio. I had already asked James Astor to help me in that respect; the two combined to produce many helpful suggestions, especially related to my tendency to condense sentences and think my audience is informed about matters with which I am familiar.

It was Donald Meltzer who started it all by suggesting that I write my autobiography but I am also indebted to Gianna Williams, who read through many of the earlier chapters.

1   THE FORDHAMS

The Fordham family were landowners and they were a sort of clan. There were numerous branches so that if you went to a party almost everyone there was a Fordham: uncles and aunts, cousins etc. They tended to intermarry and to this they attributed difficulties in their personalities. I never knew my Fordham grandparents though I was told that my grandfather was a good, supportive and liberal man and that my grandmother was much loved, especially because of her 'healing powers' through which she helped others. They begat four sons and two daughters, one of whom died early on of 'epilepsy'.

One day my uncle Ernest, whom we visited most often, walked me up a hill (called Hangman's Hill) not far from where he lived. He bade me look to the right, to the left and straight ahead over the gently undulating country: 'All that you can see is Fordham land' he said, and we walked back to his handsome house. I don't remember very well what I thought about this announcement but I suppose I thought it only natural that my family should own all the land. I don't think it surprised me for I had already noticed that labourers and others of the 'lower classes' would greet us touching their hats as they did so and shopkeepers would always be polite and provide especially good service. All that I had come to accept as an especially agreeable aspect of our visits to Odsey House near Ashwell in Hertfordshire. I liked it.

There were three brothers besides my father – they all lived in a much grander way than he. There was uncle (Sir) George Fordham, who lived in the largest house called Odsey; my family never stayed there. The house was impressive, servants were there in abundance and the large garden was well kept. Sir George was about the same size as the others but he was especially distinguished by a waxed moustache stretching out on either side of his upper lip for an inch or more. He was the eldest and as a child I found him rather remote. My only vivid memory of him was much later when he married his fourth wife (the others had died), the mother of a friend of mine at preparatory school. On one occasion we were summoned to Odsey where Uncle George 'produced' his wife as a singer. As usual it was impressive, but my mother had a much better voice than the other Mrs Fordham.

The next eldest brother was Uncle Ernest, who was much more available. He lived in an uncompleted Georgian house, Odsey House, about 200 yards from Odsey. Our family went to stay with him and were fetched from the station in a trap driven by a coachman; the luggage was brought on later. We entered the front gate to go down a short drive through magnificent beech trees with nests of rooks in them. The front door was up some steps at the foot of a blank wall, indicating where building had ceased, and one entered the hall where our hats and coats were hung. The whole house was superbly kept. It had large tall rooms on the ground floor, all panelled: the dining room was painted white, the drawing room was, I think, two shades of blue. The furniture in this part of the house was all antique, mahogany table and sideboard and Sheridan chairs in the dining-room. Apart from meals Uncle Ernest did not live in this part of the house – the drawing-room being in any case a show piece and extremely uncomfortable. The living room was down some stairs and along a passage. It was panelled in oak and had large comfortable chairs and a sofa. The big log-burning fireplace was plentifully supplied with wood which made a splendid blaze with no trouble at all. Close to this room was a capacious lavatory and ample wash-basin which I liked very much for some reason. The 'smoking room' smelt richly of wood smoke mixed with that of my uncle's pipe tobacco. I must add another delight. Each morning tea and thin bread and butter were placed beside my bed by a maid who also pulled back the curtains. There were also a large garden, two fields and a copse in which rabbits were shot after being driven from their holes by ferrets. It is small wonder that I enjoyed staying with Uncle Ernest. I felt I belonged to a very grand family, especially because there was a Fordham's bank and a Fordham's brewery, not to mention Sir George's and Uncle Sydney's farms and coal business as well.

Uncle Sydney, who owned the coal business, was the youngest of the brothers and the most human. His house was comfortable but not impressive like the other two. He was the one who took real care of his farm, which he continued to look after well, even through the agricultural depression. He owned a single cylinder Rover car, which to my delight would attain the great speed of thirty miles an hour if driven all out down hill! He married Alice, an Irish woman, of whom I became fond. She was well built and agile both in mind and body. She played golf for Ireland and was a good horsewoman. The latter talent resulted in a tragedy: when pregnant with her first child she insisted on riding against doctor's warnings – she had a miscarriage and never became pregnant again. That was sad because they would have made good parents.

Uncle Ernest was most impressed by the importance of the family, whose 'hereditary worth descends to us from a bygone hoary age', as I later found quoted in a *History of Royston*, the quote giving support to Ernest's pride. He once explained to me that no Fordham had ever sought distinction: to be a Fordham was enough – they ran the countryside and were devoted to the land. It was regarded as a lapse that my grandfather and others of the clan had departed into commerce although all the sons benefited financially and could afford to farm their land during the agricultural depression. I suppose Uncle Ernest made these points because he had married into the aristocracy and so had to boost his importance, but I did not realize that at the time. I should say that none of the three brothers was a large land-owner (they owned about 1200 acres in all). The only slight blot on the landscape was that my own family was not as affluent and grand as the Fordhams of Ashwell, or rather of Odsey as they are better described, but my parents had other merits as I shall detail later.

So much for my impressions as a child. I have not paid much attention to the reality of the family but have sought to describe the effect they had on me as a child. That impression lasted well into adult life and I was for many years given to boasting about them, to the intense irritation of others, especially my second wife, Frieda. I have overcome the habit. None the less these impressions reinforced my sense of social security, which my parents also gave me: I was a Fordham, they always made good, and I would be like them and have, as a matter of course, a sense of social responsibility.

Subsequently I learned more about them. The family had lived in East Anglia for centuries and were well known locally. It is probable that they went up and down in the social hierarchy. My brother Christopher believed that they were basically yeoman farmers, some of whom became rich and members of the 'county set'. They occasionally rose to positions of eminence, one of them becoming Bishop of Durham and later of Ely in the fourteenth century – he was said to be on Wat Tyler's black list as an enemy of the working class. Uncle George also attained eminence and was knighted. He, like other Fordhams, had a sense of social responsibility and I was once shown a list of the various prestigious positions he held in the county of Hertfordshire by a colleague, Fred Plaut. I knew that he had been chairman of the Cambridgeshire County Council and that nobody was able to dislodge him until he flew the Red Flag above the Union Jack on Labour Day. He was evicted but held on to other important posts in the county.

It was not only in the political and social field that he was distinguished. When my first wife wanted to obtain some information from the Bibliothèque Nationale in Paris she met with various prevarications until somebody there noticed that her name was Fordham and asked whether she was any relative of Sir George Fordham. On receiving an affirmative reply every facility of the library was immediately made available to her. I never understood that, for by the time I came on the scene the brothers regarded him as a not-so-amiable eccentric. It was only many years later that I heard – again from Fred Plaut, who collected maps – that Uncle George had invented the science of cartobibliography. That would have been quite beyond his brothers to understand, although I should have thought my father could have done so. Neither was Uncle Ernest without distinction of his own, for he was for many years chairman of the Fens Catchment Board and a member of Lloyd George's Agricultural Committee.

As well as all this there were fringe achievements that I heard of: Uncle George's son, Herbert, played croquet for England and won prizes at Bisley, and his daughter, Margery, played hockey for England. Then there was a cousin who was a good horseman and won more point-to-points than anybody else in England; at his funeral the hounds were brought into the church as part of the ceremony. So my Uncle Ernest's remark was probably made to emphasize that whatever Fordhams did in the world was on merit and not by graft or as the result of undue influence. That idea caused me much trouble in later years when my achievements were hailed as unusual. I could never understand that what I had done was other than what a Fordham would ordinarily do.

Besides the somewhat arrogant stance, the Fordhams regarded themselves as a bit 'mad' and Sir George illustrates what they were referring to. During World War One he was too old to join the army so he invented a regiment, presumably of older men. I used to see him returning from parade in a special uniform, presumably of his own design – he was nothing if not inventive! In his old age he let his house fall into disrepair and did not seem to use much of it; indeed, I got the impression that he lived mostly in the kitchen with his daughter, studying French railway guides – he was probably inventing a new science!

There was, however, a real basis for their concern although they did not seem to realize it, for one cousin became schizophrenic and was accommodated in Odsey, another was a lesbian and decidedly eccentric whilst Uncle Sydney developed a senile psychosis and destroyed a lot of his valuable collection of Waterford glass and antique furniture. My cousin Kathleen used to visit him and 'play' at catching horses, which, according to one of his delusions, had escaped into his garden. She seemed to think it was rather fun and even enjoyable. The idea of any Fordham being mad in the psychiatric sense was dismissed with vigour and I had a great deal of difficulty in getting a psychiatric nurse to give Uncle Sydney the continuous care he obviously needed. Kathleen once took her father, Ernest, to see an eminent psychiatrist when he was suffering from senile dementia. I expect the psychiatrist made that diagnosis, for he said he had never been spoken to by anybody in the way my cousin presumably let fly at him. She carried her father off to Odsey House where he demented under her care.

Some of those who read this manuscript have remarked on the absence of any reference either to my own parents or my brother and sister. I can only say that they featured hardly at all in my memories of these visits. The only recognition of my parents' existence is that when I slept in a room next to them, and after I had drunk the tea and eaten the sandwiches beside my bed, I would go into their room and probably got into their bed.

2 THE WORTHINGTONS

I was born in 1905, and was perhaps five years old when my parents, my brother Christopher and my sister Thea went to Switzerland for a skiing holiday. My two siblings were much older than me – five and ten years respectively – and I was judged too young to go with them. So I was sent to stay with my maternal grandparents at Broomfield, Alderley Edge in Cheshire. My grandfather Thomas Worthington and his second wife and some of his family lived in a comfortable house which he had built. When I stayed there, there were three uncles living at home: Claude, Tom and Hubert, all grown up and working in Manchester. I used to watch them, fascinated, as they stood in a row shaving in front of separate mirrors before they left the house in the morning. They brushed their faces with soap and then scratched it all off. These uncles were good fun – Claude, the eldest, was my special favourite though I can't remember why. After breakfast they rushed off to catch the train to Manchester and I remember the excitement of being allowed to go with them once to see them off at the station.

When my brother and sister were there on other occasions, we children used to pelt the uncles with rotten apples. The uncles went into the loft above the carriage house where there was a large window through which they poked their heads and threw apples back at us. There was a disused copper mine which they took us down. There was much accumulated water to be negotiated in the often narrow tunnels of this mine. Another adventure that they

Broomfield

engineered was to take me up to the 'wizard's cave' where I could peer down and talk to the wizard who answered in a gruff voice – I was credulous enough to believe he was real. Another illustration of this was my firm belief in Father Christmas up to the age of eleven. He invariably dispensed goodies at Broomfield and once Uncle Hubert was absent when Father Christmas arrived. After he had gone Uncle Hubert rushed into the room excitedly telling how he had been asked to look after the reindeer whilst Father Christmas went into the house. Any doubts I might have harboured were immediately allayed.

Grandfather also had a sense of fun; he was a very dignified old gentleman with white hair and a beard. In the morning he came to breakfast in a dressing-gown and a skull-cap. I would sit on his knee in front of the porridge, onto which he directed a stream of golden syrup poured from a spoon: he held it high in the air so that he could make patterns on the food. I think it was granny (Mater as she was called by her children) who, perhaps noticing me gazing at him, said 'Do you think grandpa is very old?', at which I exclaimed in indignation, 'My grandpa is not old he is quite new!', to the great delight of the old gentleman. I expect everybody else laughed. Grandfather was not only fun; he was also powerful and possibly dangerous. His power was located in his study. It was at the end of a long passage and nobody was allowed into it. At the entry into the passage furthest from the room there was, either in reality or in my imagination, I don't know which, a line which it was forbidden to cross. I can remember looking into the study since the door was sometimes open and once I put my foot over the line, only to draw it back hastily lest my crime be discovered.

On Sundays the family went to the Methodist church in a carriage. We sat up in the gallery in the front row. The great event was to be given the princely sum of six pence to put in the collection. A large bowl was handed round and my grandfather put in a golden guinea. There was a family story about this. It appears that on one occasion Uncle Hubert thought of a brilliant notion: he would put in his six pence and take out the golden guinea, which he did. It is characteristic of that family that it was retold with quiet humour so that I felt sure he was not punished.

Foremost amongst ceremonial occasions, beside going to church, was Christmas dinner. The table was covered with nuts, sweetmeats and other treats and the children were instructed to run round it between courses so as to shake the food down and make more room for what was to come. That I did and ate heartily. Another ceremony was New Year's Eve. When I first stayed in the house I was deemed too young to participate but later I was allowed to stay up and drink punch with the uncles in a room at the top of one of the two towers, which were on either side of the front door of the house. There we saw in the New Year.

Another memory: we went to inspect a cotton mill owned by a step-uncle. I was impressed by the rattle of the machinery – the looms – and by the way my step-uncle went round and talked with his employees (some of whom were children); he seemed to have such a happy relationship with them.

Going to Broomfield was always a happy time, so that when my family went away to Switzerland I do not remember missing them much. There was a large lawn in front of the house; it sloped steeply

Thomas Worthington

enough for me to toboggan down it. I enjoyed that. Being left
behind, however, must have had its effect because although later I
was good at games and sports I could never ski – ever: a stemming
turn was beyond my competence.

So much for my memories of the Worthingtons as a child – all of
them are good and had a certain glamour, centring round
grandfather. My impression was of a different kind of family from
the Fordhams. Both families were patriarchal in structure but the
wives of the Worthingtons never complained of their husbands
whilst, with the exception of my mother, all Fordham wives did so.
Apart from the house and gardens, which were impressive enough,
the Worthingtons had no land, no history and were not a clan as
the Fordhams were. So they were all more personal and human.

I learned more about my mother's family later on. My grandfather
had two families and there were, I believe, six children by each
wife. His first was related to Scott, editor of the Manchester
Guardian, which gave her a reflected glory. I understood from his
daughter, my Aunt Edie, that the second brood was not up to the
first. The second family went in for 'commerce', unlike the first, to
which my mother and aunt belonged, and though Uncle Hubert
(second family) became a good architect he was in a different class
from Uncle Percy (first family), who became the first president of
the Royal Institute of Architects from the provinces. He was also a
good classical scholar.

I was given to understand that my grandfather was one of the
most eminent architects in the north of England and greatly glorified
the city of Manchester with his buildings. He also painted good
water-colours, and my mother became a singer and Aunt Edie a
painter. I suppose it was the professional, artistic and literary
connections which gave the first family a feeling of superiority over
the second. All I understood from it was that I belonged to the better
family.

A surprising streak in grandfather's character was exhibited
when Aunt Edie left home to study painting with Hercommer. My
grandfather disinherited her because she would not come home.
Why should he do that? A possible answer is as follows: the family
lived in an area, Alderley Edge, popular with the Manchester
establishment. His house was big and my grandmother behaved in

the proper way: dressing well, entertaining, making calls on neighbours and possessing a silver tray for visiting cards (which impressed me most). The establishment was, however, suspicious. To have a daughter mixed up with art, living alone in France did not conform with their ideas of what was proper behaviour. Moreover, when grandfather travelled to France it was said that he was mixed up with some revolution there. It was all somewhat romantic and so irregular. I cannot believe, however, that he was so much worried about his reputation as concerned to preserve his daughter's virginity. In support of this view is the fact that my mother was trained as a professional singer and I never heard that grandfather stood in her way about that, but she never left home except to marry. I am glad to say that he must have relented, for Aunt Edie subsequently had enough to live on.

Returning to the two families, whilst it was true that the groups held themselves apart there were overlaps: Uncle Hubert was fond of my mother. He used to come and stay with us and sketched houses in which we might live. He was 'matey' whereas Uncle Percy (first family) was prestigious. On one occasion when he was leaving, my mother suggested I might go to the front gate to say goodbye – it might be to my advantage. It was: he gave me half a crown.

After the First World War, Broomfield no longer featured in my life. There were, however, two aunts who were kind to me. There was Aunt Letty (first family), who had three sons, two of whom were twins of about my age. I went on holidays with them at Hythe and much enjoyed catching mackerel in my hands as the fishermen hauled their nets full of fish onto the beach. However, it was Aunt Edie with whom I formed a firm friendship. After she left Broomfield she lived mostly in London: Kensington, Campden Hill and last of all Chelsea. She never went on much with her painting but she was a brilliant copyist and was once invited by a famous gallery to go to Russia and copy some of their classical paintings for reproduction in Great Britain. She never did so being, I suppose, too old. She had a very clear and well-ordered mind and my second wife, Frieda, was astonished when Aunt Edie gave her a concise account of the essence of existentialism, which had previously bewildered her. At one time Aunt Edie was librarian under the secretary of the

Anthroposophical Society, R.G.S. Mead. No doubt that gave her a chance to apply her mental abilities. My parents were much incensed at the way Mead was said to have exploited her. She was also interested in spiritualism and once, when I was grown up, invited me to meet a medium. That was not a success. As I was a sceptic the medium could not operate well in the atmosphere I created. He ended up by saying that there was an important message for me between the pages of one of the books in my aunt's library. As there were well over a hundred books on her shelves that was the end of our meeting. I understood much more of the importance Aunt Edie gave to spiritualism when I sat beside her death-bed and listened to her rather indistinct conversations with the spirits – she died peacefully with their aid.

Mother

3   My Parents

I don't remember my parents much, or my brother and sister, until we moved to Hillcroft, a house in the village of Steep in Hampshire, when I was about six. Then I knew that I loved my mother passionately. It was a passion that burst through explicitly from time to time and from which she tactfully extracted herself. It once burst through when she came to bid me goodnight dressed up for a dinner party. She looked absolutely ravishing and I flung my arms round her neck like a devoted lover. At other times I knew it when I got into her bed in the morning, nestling against her breasts and once when burrowing down under the bedclothes I tried to get up her legs in the direction of her genitals – she crossed her legs so she knew what I was after. Then there were the times when she sat in front of the mirror combing her hair, which fell down to her waist, and she imperiously tossed it into order with a large tortoiseshell comb. Again I loved her when she read to me in the bathroom before bed sometimes. I especially liked her to read Daniel in the lion's den from the Bible. She also read to me at other times and one book called *The Little Prince* I knew so well that when my mother turned a page, I could quite often get on with the next sentence before she read on. Other pleasurable occasions were when I sat on her knee whilst she and the cook worked out the meals for the day. She used to doodle on a piece of paper she had before her on the kitchen table. In retrospect I suspect she made mandalas.

But that was only half the picture; she was puzzled about why I was the naughty one of the family. 'I can't understand why you are so naughty,' she once said, 'Thea and Chris are not like that'. I used to abuse her from time to time, mostly because I thought her stupid and she once retorted: 'I will not be spoken to like that'. My relief was immediate and I wished that she would put her foot down more often and stop my compulsion, but on the whole she did not. Once, on my seventh birthday, the family went for a picnic in the beech woods and I behaved very well so that the outing was a joy for everybody. When we got home mother said: 'Don't you see how nice it has been?' I had to agree. She was a perceptive woman and considering my behaviour in retrospect, my position was much more that of an only child competing unsuccessfully with a group of adults, than one of three children.

Then there was mother's music. She conducted the village choir, which used to compete at an annual music festival and Steep invariably came first or second, to my reflected glory: what a mother I had. Above all there was her singing. She had a beautiful soprano voice and at one time she took singing lessons. Her teacher came to our house and strange preliminary noises came out of the drawing-room first – then she would burst into song. One day I was in the kitchen with the cook and after the usual introduction my mother broke into song: it was 'Voi che sapete'. The cook and I listened entranced as the beautiful crystal sounds flowed over the air. All work stopped until she had finished when the cook said: 'Your mother has a much better voice than her teacher'. I liked her laconic remark.

Mother wanted to convey to us children her love of music and part of doing so was to hope the three of us would make a trio: my sister was to play the violin, my brother the cello and I was to play the piano. Only my sister developed some competence which she retained in later life. Mother tried to teach me the piano. She was a competent pianist but it must have been a hard task, for my fingers would not do what was required, to my great distress. Once I ended up hitting the keys with my fists. Apart from my performance, however, she had some success in that she gave me a catholic love of music, which has been a source of much enjoyment. I never achieved competence on the piano but I obtained pleasure from struggling with the easier parts of Bach, Mozart, Beethoven and

Chopin. I never met anybody else who liked my efforts and Frieda, also the child of a singer, positively disliked them so that I eventually gave up playing altogether.

There were two other occasions when my mother's beauty ravished me: one was when she came to sports day at my preparatory school. I was apprehensive about her coming because of the affluence of some of my friends' parents. I waited outside the front door of the school from which she would emerge: she was just so lovely that I at once threw myself into her arms. The other occasion that I was entranced by her was just before her death. She was seriously ill and I too was in bed with earache. She came into my room in her dressing-gown and sat down and I lay there enjoying her. The next day she was dead and the family went to see her corpse – she looked so tranquil.

Contrary to what might be expected I am deeply grateful for that last memory of her visit to my bedside – it meant that my 'naughtiness' had not harmed or damaged her. But it did leave me with a ghost, an enduring memory, and as I later realized also a terrible one.

My mother was not always that lovely woman: walking in the garden I would survey her heavy hips and buttocks and think how different she was down below. Sometimes I would arrive in her bedroom to find her looking worn and surrounded with bottles and sprays. That was when she had been having an attack of asthma. As I write this I at once think of her sitting in front of the mirror combing her long flowing hair – even now I cannot think anything bad about her without immediately recalling something good. Today I have two pictures of her: one is an exquisite line drawing of her as a young woman, the other is of her in middle age, her beauty gone, and that I like best because she is a human being.

Mother loved flowers and knew all the names of those growing in the garden. The gardener worked hard to have all those that she loved planted in the borders and flower-beds. Because of her love, expressed in her knowledge, I could not remember the names of flowers till very late in life.

So far I have depicted my relation to my mother as I remember it. Those memories are inevitably given significance retrospectively and they are organized in a way a child could not have done. That is largely due to my analytic experience but I have not included that in my description, since I am only trying to depict my growing consciousness. Nevertheless I believe that analysis has contributed to that truth.

I will now add more about my mother from what I was told; it is not direct knowledge but hearsay. It appears that when young she used to sing as an amateur at concerts and at one of these Cecil Sharp, the musician famous for his researches into folk songs, was present. He offered to train her as a professional singer, so a career was opened to her. I do not know what happened next or who trained her, but after my sister was born the family went out to Berlin so that my mother could study music there. So there seems no doubt that she followed up Cecil Sharp's proposal. She never sang professionally after I was born, but after my father's death I found some newspaper cuttings which reported very favourably indeed on my mother's performances, to which I remember her referring. One of them praised her voice but criticized her 'attack' in some passages of a Bach Cantata. Probably it was the birth of us children and her contracting asthma that ended her professional career. It was none the less remarkable that at the end of the Victorian age she should have been allowed to pursue a professional career at all. It is perhaps a tribute to grandfather and my father that she began to sing professionally – her love of music was serious and devoted.

My father was very different from my mother; there was a romantic flavour to him. He was a great help on walks for when I complained at being left behind, being much the youngest, he did not grumble as my brother and sister did but rode me on his shoulders and so we went along together. He was strong and a great talker, at which I used to protest but that did not deflect him at all. He told me stories about himself. He told me how he had been round the world. In India he had stayed in a palace in the middle of a lake as the guest of a maharaja. He caught malaria there and when he left it was on the only white trotting elephant in India. All that was made real by the numerous Indian costumes in which we children used to dress up. In addition there was the picture of the palace which hung on the wall of a room. After that he went on to Japan – he talked about the gardens, which he much admired, and

Father

how he had climbed up the sacred mountain Fujiyama. He possessed numerous Japanese prints, single ones and others in books. He knew how to make a small Japanese garden with dwarf trees and shrubs in it. He also gave lectures on Japan and showed slides of the country.

He had a most delightful capacity to engage my emotions. Sometimes he would sing: 'Old mother talky talky/ too long I stay/ Dinna wed another darkie/ while I am away'. *Brer Rabbit* also fascinated me when read by him and also *Uncle Remus*. There was his study where he was writing a book. It went forward very slowly and as far as I know never got written – it was to be a *History of British Agriculture*. He had already written a *Short History*, which seems to have become a classic for it went on selling for many years. The study was not awe-inspiring like my grandfather's but it had a certain numinosity. But then my father was not awe-inspiring – he was to be admired and loved and was sometimes infuriating.

There were a number of activities in which he engaged us children, including going for walks and on bicycle rides. I could not participate in these at first but my father would let me ride on his handlebars. Later I had a bicycle of my own and made good use of it, though I never went on their long expeditions which lasted for days on end. The family also played tennis but I was so far behind that I despaired of catching them up, so that I was never much good at it. My father was keen enough on tennis to make a court and I joined in the making of it. Since the soil was clay it was necessary to make a drainage system under the surface, which, of course, had to be carefully covered with rather special South Downs turf and rolled regularly.

Another activity was keeping rights of way open. There was a Mr Trevor Batty who was keen to close some of them and he put up barricades across them. We assiduously removed them. My father contested his right to put them up at the meetings of the Parish Council, of which he was a member. A further activity was pumping water: all of it had to be pumped from a rainwater tank up to the top of the house, for there was no mains supply as there is nowadays; each of us had to pump twenty times each day. I complained about that from time to time but was not let off the chore.

What discipline was needed in our home, and it was not much, Father implemented. It was he who removed me from the dining-room when I behaved too badly at meal times. Once on a memorable occasion – it was in the drawing-room – he picked up my mother's cherished conducting baton and hit me over the right shoulder – the baton broke. It is the only time I remember my mother being really angry. I do not know why he did that but many years later he told me that I was a most infuriating child. From my point of view he was a powerful and enjoyable person and I was proud to have such a father, except when he talked too much. That he would do especially when guests came who were interested in his ideas. They were largely meaningless to me and there is a story which certainly expresses my view of the matter, though I have no memory of it. It appears that the family were on a walk with one of the guests and I was being carried on my father's shoulders. He was expounding on one of his favourite themes and in the middle of it I hit him on the head and exclaimed: 'You talk and talk and you don't know what you are talking about!' The talk proceeded as before, though no doubt with a slight intermission.

The other feature of my father was his absolute reliability in a crisis. He invariably got the point and knew what to do and if there was anything I wanted to do he would help if he could. He seemed always to know the right people to approach. I will relate examples of what he did later.

In his childhood and I presume adolescence as well, my father must have lived at Odsey but when grown up he was not left any property and he abandoned the land, except in the sense that he engaged actively in agricultural politics and writing about agriculture. How did this come about? It appears that his intellectual ability had much to do with it. As landed gentry, the male members of the family would have gone through the rigmarole of going to school – the senior branch went to Eton – but they were primarily interested in their estates or farms and in running the countryside. That did not apply to Sir George, who neglected his farm and was exploited by his bailiff. My father distinguished himself at school and the headmaster wanted him to remain there for another year so that he could compete for a scholarship in mathematics at Cambridge. My grandfather asked about this proposal but my father firmly said he did not want a scholarship and wanted to go to university and become a wrangler (a wrangler was someone who attained a first in part one of the tripos). My grandfather backed him and he succeeded in his ambition. I think that incident was characteristic. My father knew what he wanted to do and did it, the necessary support of his father being granted. He had the means to do as he wished and it mostly continued like that throughout his life because of the financial support left to him. That was my experience of him and that attitude has been influential in my own life.

There is now a gap in my father's history until he married my mother and lived in Birmingham. He was then a solicitor and businessman, being chairman of a flourishing laundry. He also developed other interests, for example in 'arts and crafts' (what is now called art nouveau) but there is no indication that he opened a gallery or shop as he did later in London. He formed a Land Club which promulgated a policy for the revival of agriculture and it was probably in this period that he wrote his first book, *Mother Earth*, which was published in 1908. He seems to have had some success with his political efforts and no doubt the Chamberlains, whom he knew personally, were sympathetic but in the end he was defeated – being a Fabian could not have been helpful. As far as I was concerned, however, attending conferences of the Fabian Society provided good holidays, one of which – in Wales – I especially remember. By and large my father was evidently set on a successful and lucrative career. Uncle Sydney was most puzzled when he threw it all up, as in his opinion 'he was well set to become town clerk of Birmingham'.

I believe the reason for this was my mother's health. She had developed asthma and the doctors pronounced that it was bad for her to live in Birmingham and the family should move. So the family was transported to 1 Tor Gardens, Campden Hill in London, where I was born. My father then ran a gallery and shop called The Artificers Guild, located in Maddox Street. It was probably during this time that he made contact with the world of literature, of which Edward Garnett and his wife Constance, who translated the Russian authors, would have been the centre. The family had some sort of relationship with Conrad, Hudson and Galsworthy. Galsworthy was evidently fond of my mother and he became my godfather. My parents' connections must have been quite wide, and not only with writers, for I found a photograph inscribed by Dusa, the famous Italian actress, amongst my father's collection of photographs. When it was that he collected such a number of eminent and semi-eminent friends I do not know, but it was so, and when information or help from them was required it was, as far as I knew, always available. There was one remark by my father which may be relevant. He once said that at the gallery people used to come to listen to what he had to say. Presumably he either gave lectures or, more likely, developed discussion groups.

I have said enough to indicate my father's extremely complex, interesting, and to my mind admirable, character. When asked what my father did I was always nonplussed because he did so many things. My answer to the enquiry about him was that he was a gentleman and did very much what he liked and that was many things. There were, however, two constants: his devotion to my mother and to the cause of agriculture. As a father he was also constantly there if help was needed, but he very much led his own life and so left us children free to develop our own.

I was fortunate in my parents but their merits also caused a quandary since I was the bad one and very much the youngest (I mostly dealt with my siblings by not having much to do with them but admiring both of them). So it took me a long time to discover that I had real worth equal to theirs in my own way.

I was born at 1 Tor Gardens, Campden Hill in London on 4 August 1905, while my mother was in the middle of a severe asthma attack, as I learned later. Perhaps because of my mother's health the family soon moved into the country, to a house near Limpsfield in Surrey. My early memories give an inconsequent and disconnected impression but the house seems to have represented something solid and containing. Other houses to which the family moved later had the same feel about them.

This first one seemed to be a large comfortable one with polished wood floors, furniture and staircase. I remember the staircase particularly; it also was of polished wood and I slipped on it and cut my chin on a stair. My Aunt Edie solicitously put a dressing over it – some 'new skin'. Though I probably had a shock I do not remember it – only the blood and my aunt's care, which gave me satisfaction. I have the scar on my chin to the present day. The rooms were convenient for climbing round without touching the floor, but the exercise was difficult enough to evoke my ingenuity and occasional worry about falling off some insufficiently large protuberance on the wall on which I was balancing. Outside the house there were large lawns to play on and a semicircular rockery, which I found impressive but did not climb over; I expect that was prohibited.

I recollect that the family were expected to go for walks: we went out of the drive, turned to the left and walked down a hill. At the bottom was a pumping station for water – we did not go in there but walked back up the hill making for home. I also went down a hill to a nursery school in Limpsfield. I had no objections to going there and, I suppose, got on quite well with Miss Featherstonehaw, the teacher, except on one occasion. I believe that is the first clear memory of my life: there was a ritual game to which she introduced us based on the poem 'Three blind mice'. Each child played the part of the farmer's wife and was given a small stick, representing a knife, with which he or she could pretend to cut off the tails of the other children (the mice). When it came to my turn I became so enthusiastic and excited that I had to be restrained.

Another early memory was of my nanny, a nice-looking young woman for whose loving, disciplinary capacities I evidently had respect. Every afternoon I was expected to rest in bed. How often I did not do that I do not know but I was once caught. I was sitting on the window-sill surveying the garden when I heard a suspicious noise. Round the door of my room came my nanny's face: 'Oooh . . . ', she said. By the time she came into the room I was back in bed. I do not remember any dire consequences arising from this episode but I suspect I was more careful afterwards about obeying the regulation.

I cannot date these memories nor do I know how long my family lived in that house but as I grew older, perhaps four or five, I partook more in family events. I became more aware of my brother Chris and my sister Thea. We formed a troupe of 'three little savages', of which I have very vague recollections but there are photographs of us to remind me. I was told that we found a dead hedgehog, wrapped it up in clay and baked it, but I do not remember that, though I remember a wigwam that we built. My sister was the leader in our activities and once we went carol-singing, collecting money for ourselves – our parents made us return it; such behaviour was not to be countenanced.

A family outing often took place on Sundays (it may also have occurred on other days of the week). We all walked over to a house called 'The Cearn' where Constance Garnett lived. Sometimes her husband Edward or her son David, who was fond of my sister, were there also. David was very beautiful and seemed to me like a god. I do not remember any of the occupants of that house taking much notice of me but I do remember its smell: it was of burnt wood from the capacious fireplace in the main room. Climbing beech trees that surrounded 'The Cearn' was a great delight. It was my first introduction to climbing and I liked to reach a spot so high that I was lost in a sea of green and could not see the ground.

Looking back over this period it is remarkable that neither of my parents featured much. I can be rather sure that my father would have placed me on his shoulders during the longish walk to 'The Cearn' and I can remember my mother putting me to bed and telling me that four angels guarded me during the night, 'Two at my feet and two at my head'. That was nice and I assumed it as my right. Yet somewhere I must have had an idea that the angels would be useful against a danger that I had not known of, but my mother did.

There is one other memory which I must record because it has a bearing on the course my analysis took in later years. There was a very large man who used to visit us. I believe he came to sing with my mother, but he impressed me very much because of his size. He seemed a sort of giant; his name was Godwin Baynes. Subsequently he became my Jungian analyst but he had no connection with psychology or Jung when I knew him as a child.

5   REMOVALS

A lot of packing up was going on and it continued until we left the first house in my life when I was three or four years old. I do not remember leaving but I do remember arriving at Clapham Junction. (I am convinced that I was told and remembered the title of that station at that time.) My mother and I were together, I was sitting on her knee in a railway carriage looking out of the window. I thought we were at the centre of the world and all trains came to Clapham Junction where our train had stopped. I felt important and secure.

Our first port of call was a house in Hampshire reminiscent of the house in Limpsfield we had come from. It was on a hill and I liked looking at the view of the countryside. There was a man staying with us. He was a great help in building bridges. I had been given a constructional toy: pieces of wood made so that they could be fitted together to make a large range of objects. I wanted to build a bridge and was in difficulties. The man joined in and all went well – I do not remember whether the bridge was ever completed because I had become much more interested in the man than the bridge. Sadly, he soon went away but I do not think I felt distress at his departure. His name was Julian Huxley.

Near us lived other interesting people. There was a family we visited. They lived in an agreeable house surrounded by trees at the foot of the downs. The wife presided in the background so it was the father and son who interested me. The son was rather mysterious and I did not succeed in making a relationship with him. He was older than me and, like my brother, probably thought I was not worth taking much notice of. His father, however, had a room of his own in which there were a lot of fluids and pieces of metal on which he scratched – I understood that in that way he made pictures and he kindly showed me how it was done. I forget the details but it involved putting the metal in trays of fluid – now I know he was making etchings. His name was Muirhead Bone.

Soon we moved to an older and smaller house, Berryfield Cottage, although it was somewhat larger than a cottage. Near it a mansion was being built by a Mr Trevor Batty. Down by the entrance was a large fir tree, good for climbing, and there was an outside earth closet which was to become important. I was fond of a girl of about my own age and we enjoyed each other's company. As we became more intimate we interested ourselves in each other's faeces and used to go into the earth closet; I especially enjoyed the prettiness of her buttocks and her being rather slow in expelling her faeces: 'It's coming, it's coming' she would say in encouragement. Suddenly our relationship was interrupted. She did not come to see me and when I went down to her home near by she was 'not at home' and so it went on. I sought her but she was never to be found and she faded out of my life except as a cherished memory. I just accepted her absence as incomprehensible although later I concluded that my mother had discovered what was going on and combined with the girl's mother to put a stop to it. I do not seem to have been especially miserable, though I was hurt and wandered about disconsolately trying to find her. That incident reverberated in my relations with other girls and adult women, whom I either idealized, or feared would go away if I became too close.

Other reminiscences whilst living in Berryfield Cottage were of harvesting and the fun of bouncing about in the corn fields or on top of the cart on which the straw was collected. I do not remember other members of the family particularly, but when we children all caught measles we lived in the same room and I was then close to both my brother and sister for a short period. On one holiday in Wales my mother found a cook, who came back with us to Berryfield Cottage, and made especially good bread. The country surrounding us was very beautiful and the family custom of taking walks through the woods and over the South Downs continued.

In this chapter I have continued to record a cluster of memories which do not seem to have much to do with each other. Yet they are ones that have special significance in a number of respects. First of all there was the girl whose significance I have mentioned; then there was Julian Huxley and Muirhead Bone, both of whom were or became important, Huxley as a biologist and Bone as an artist. I do not think I knew their merits when a child but I knew that each was somebody special – somebody of unusual quality, just as my family was. That capacity for recognition has persisted through my life and on the whole has proved reliable; it did not apply to me. I was nothing special, I only basked in reflected glory. However, there was the incident at Clapham Junction, sitting on my mother's knee, when I certainly felt important. It was significant also in a different way because there was an intimation of a larger self in the Jungian sense.

Many years later when I went to Baynes for analysis, I learned about mandalas and I made pictures of them – they seemed to me like my childhood experience at Clapham Junction. They seemed even more like it when 'working', as we put it then, with my second analyst, Hilde Kirsch. One day years later my second wife, Frieda, and I went into the lecture room in the Zurich Institute when Jung held his seminars: hanging on the wall were a number of white mandalas and Frieda remarked, 'Just look at all those breasts!' Being at that time a good Jungian I was deeply shocked; how could she say such a thing!

Again later on, when working in supervision with a Kleinian psychoanalyst, I told him about the experience at Clapham Junction and he said that my feeling was that of a baby at the breast. That embodied the experience further and much good came of it: many events fell into place but in particular it helped in building a bridge for me between Jungian and Kleinian experiences. I say that in an emotional and personal, rather than intellectual, sense.

6   HILLCROFT

I am continuing to give prominence to where we lived because that was a focal point for me as a child. The next house, called 'Hillcroft', was in Steep, near Petersfield in Hampshire. The family moved there in 1910 when I was five years old and we stayed there for seven years. Hillcroft was less beautiful than the previous houses. In front of it was a thick laurel hedge; it expressed our exclusiveness. The house was on the village street and no longer in the country so a barrier was needed to keep out the riff-raff. There were entrance gates: a small one through which guests and family entered and a large one about six feet high and rather more across which was the entrance to the outbuildings – a gardener's shed and a bigger one which must have been to lodge a carriage that we did not have, therefore it housed our bicycles and other objects.

Since the house was rather small my father built on extra rooms at the back and I much enjoyed climbing up the scaffolding to watch and talk to the builders. When finished it enlarged the kitchen, scullery and larder on the ground floor and made a bedroom for my brother and a playroom for me. Beside this extension a sizeable garden was constructed in the shape of a cross, and also a tennis court. There was no water laid on as it is nowadays. The rainwater from the roof was collected in a tank and then pumped up to another tank in the attic. Hot water was provided by a magnificent kitchen stove with numerous exciting dampers. There was also our own sewage system and I think the gardener dealt with that by using the products on the garden or otherwise disposing of them.

We lived here for a relatively long time, and it is here that my parents came onto my memory screen as I have described them. The Odsey Fordhams and the Worthington family reached clearer definition in my mind, though the first memory of Broomfield came earlier. My life during these seven years was predominantly happy although there were no friends of my own age group and my brother and sister were scarcely siblings to be companions. It was the community there which was agreeable: besides the family there was the cook, the gardener and a man next door called Edward Thomas, who I subsequently discovered was a poet. He gave me two large volumes on some subject I could not understand and I never read them. The gardener was keen on cricket and cleaned the boots in a covered place outside the kitchen. There we followed the fortunes of my cricket heroes Hobbs and Wooley. He was also of interest because he tried to breed a yellow flowering sweet pea: he cross-fertilized a white pea with the pollen from yellow lupins, without, I fear, any success. Other interests of mine were constructing model railways and running steam engines powered with methylated spirits – they would run off the rails and go up in flames (easily put out, I am glad to say). The railways became quite complicated, going up hills and through tunnels. Besides these activities I was very much amused by shooting chickens in the bottom with my air gun; I recognized it was cruel and soon desisted. We also had dogs. The first was a dachshund called Pan. I was very much upset when he died whilst the family was on holiday. He was replaced by a beautiful white Samoyed whom I loved also, although he had a liking for catching and killing chickens. That did not bother me but he had to be shut up in his run with a dead chicken round his neck. Another occupation was breeding white mice. I eventually got rid of them by letting them run free in the garden in which they soon lost themselves.

My brother and sister soon went as day children to Bedales, the coeducational school nearby, so I saw even less of them. My parents had progressive ideas on education and it was, I think, a good school. I was at first too young to go to the preparatory school and was sent to a small one in Petersfield – as far as I remember I enjoyed it but it must have been a considerable labour taking me backwards and forwards to the town, which was two miles away. In those days motorcars were a rarity and we did not possess one, so I must have been taken there and back on a bicycle. When I was old enough I went to Bedales preparatory school. There I had my first experience of elementary arithmetic and much enjoyed the learning of tables, adding up, multiplying and dividing – I found it quite fascinating to see what could be done with numbers. I also found that I was good at football: it gave me much delight to dribble down the field evading attempts to tackle me. In addition I was exhilarated by gymnastics, especially as there was a pretty gym mistress who appreciated my prowess and massaged my feet on the grounds that I was becoming flat-footed.

It was in this period that I recollect being naughty. I attacked my mother critically, behaved badly at meal times and had to be removed from the room. I climbed over the roof and broke tiles and so on. I also complained a great deal, especially on walks, during which I tended to lag behind so that my brother and sister thought me a nuisance. I would not think of that as being naughty but perhaps my parents did.

It was, perhaps, in an unconscious effort to control or channel my aggression in socially acceptable ways that I developed a fervent desire to join the Navy. That was the first and only ambition that I harboured until I decided to become an analyst. My desire was supported by my liking for sailing and enjoyment of rough seas when on Channel crossings – the family went for holidays in France from time to time. It was also the case that we lived near the naval dockyard at Portsmouth and I could watch the naval vessels sailing in and out. On one occasion we visited Nelson's battleship, the Victory, and saw the copper plaque marking the spot at which Nelson fell during the battle of Trafalgar. But most of all it was fantasy that fed my ambition. I studied a book, *Janes Fighting Ships*, in which there were pictures of destroyers that went at thirty-six knots and I imagined them ploughing through the sea sending up flaming sheets of water from their bows; besides this there were huge battleships with twelve-, and a few with fifteen-, inch guns. Round these I fashioned fantasies of fierce battles, with enemy ships being sunk and the British fleet triumphing. Britannia rules the waves and preserves the empire which I surveyed with pride in maps of the world showing red over large parts of it – red being the colour of British possessions. Today I have no regrets that my omnipotent fantasies were not fulfilled and am grateful to my parents for not standing against them.

As it was, my father, who always seemed to know the right person to consult, found that no boy from Bedales would be accepted for the Navy so he found out where I should continue my education. There was a school which specialized in preparing boys for the Navy. The headmaster had two brothers who were admirals. That was a strong recommendation so there I went. Emsworth House was a conventional preparatory school, with a headmaster who made most of us boys feel safe and understood. It must have been terrible, however, if you got in his bad books. When he became furious his moustache bristled and he carried you off to his bedroom where you were soundly beaten. He was quite free in his use of the cane but seldom administered more than four strokes of varying weight. We boys were rather proud of our marks and compared their size and the degree of bruising. I do not think there was anything humiliating about it; indeed it was all taken in good part. However, I was not in his bad books and never got into trouble with mathematics because it was my best subject. Bud, as we called the headmaster, took that subject and I vividly remember one boy being picked up by the scruff of the neck and having his nose rubbed in the blackboard as he repeatedly failed to answer questions correctly.

Besides Bud there was his brother, who was a dyspeptic. He taught French and required periodic refills of the hot-water bottle which he held against his stomach to ease his discomfort – we exploited this need as much as we could. The matron was a good-natured aggressive woman called Gee, whose care was combined with an admixture of bullying. Physical training was conducted by an ex-soldier, a boxer with a bruiser's face who used to invite us to hit it. One lashed out as hard as possible but the face was never there! He must have been a good boxer, at any rate he thought so and we believed his stories about being champion of the Indian army. Another enjoyable feature of the school was the cook, a warm-hearted woman who had her favourites. She let us go into the kitchen to toast our bedtime ration of bread. After we had done so she would chase us out of her domain with a toasting fork, perhaps retaining a special boy. The rest of us would peer through the hatch enviously to survey her giving her chosen boy some special goodies. She was a good cook and her food was always appreciated, though during the war the helpings grew rather small owing to the rationing. From her I learned about making mayonnaise, which she prepared for parents' day. There was one other event at Emsworth House; it may seem somewhat trivial but it was a great boost to my self-esteem. An actress friend of Bud's came down to the school and I got on well with her. She remarked on my beautiful manners – so I found I could behave well and be appreciated by a woman I did not know.

The war brought considerable change. The gardener left to join the army and sadly never came back; the maid left to become a nurse; the cook also departed, though later. My father was overcome with war fever and since he was too old to join the army, he joined the British Red Cross; more of this later. Naturally I was keen on the war and Kitchener's 'knock out blow'. I was given a weekly paper called *The Illustrated War News*. The jingoistic enthusiasm was, in retrospect, quite terrible and I cannot do better than illustrate the sentiment at the time by quoting an entry in our visitors' book written by my maternal grandmother. She stayed with us between 22 and 25 May 1915, which she noted adding 'Including Empire day' and continuing with a citation from Mrs W. Archer: 'The magnificent rally of the Empire to the flag has shown that Empire is no empty word, but a living beneficent reality. And above all, the youth of the nation has sprung to arms with superb alacrity, a generous self-devotion, and one can imagine nothing more touching or beautiful'. Of my grandmother's three sons, two were severely wounded, one of them crippled for life; the third, Claude, my favourite uncle, was killed after winning the DSO and bar – he left me £50 in his will, a small consolation in my sadness at his loss.

As a volunteer in the Red Cross my father was sent to the south of France, where he was instructed to organize a party for some aristocrat. He promptly refused, saying he had not joined up to arrange parties for civilians but to further the war effort by nursing the wounded. He was equally promptly put in detention and then sent back to England. Undeterred he joined the French Red Cross, was given a much more attractive uniform and arrived at Ris-Orandis Military Hospital where he could nurse soldiers to his heart's content – my brother joined him there for a short period. My father also worked in Boulogne, where he found good companionship but was bombed by German aeroplanes, if I remember correctly.

When the servants went away my mother and I made a good combination. She was either very tactful or else she knew very little about cooking. I suspect the latter. For my part I had learned bits and pieces of that art from the cook before she left, and could manage the range. Whether it was my mother's tact or not it came about that I took a considerable part in the cooking and I was proud of the result. I was once left to cook the Christmas dinner: turkey and two stuffings, baked potatoes and vegetables followed by plum pudding and mince pies. I also knew how to make puff pastry and cakes, though the one I made to take back to school was a disaster: it was made from black market white flour and the texture was good – unfortunately all the raisins and sultanas had sunk to the bottom. That fact became apparent when the cake was cut and distributed. The boys laughed a bit but I suppose they ate it up, for it was tasty. Besides cooking I helped with cleaning, distempering and some interior decorations and so forth.

After some time finances became a problem. The railways in South America were nationalized and as we had investments in them our income was reduced. Mother wrote to Dad and he returned to England. At first he tried being a schoolmaster but that was not a success since he could not keep order. So he joined the Ministry of Labour where he got on well, but which meant our living in London. We moved to a flat on Campden Hill where we stayed till the war ended. During it the zeppelins came over London and I wanted to look out of the window to see them dropping bombs – my mother drew me firmly back from the glass. No bombs fell near us and I never saw one of these huge airships. I felt some reflected glory from my sister, who was in the 'secret service'; her work was very 'hush hush' and she could not tell us what she did. My brother remained at school until he was old enough to join the army. Great efforts were made to get him into the artillery. They were successful but fortunately just as he was being sent to France the armistice was signed and we sighed with relief.

It was soon after the war ended that I went for my interview with the admirals. I enjoyed meeting them but they asked me where the magnetic pole was located; I did not know and asked them where it was – one of them told me. I passed the interview, one of 30 out of 300 applicants. I was measured for a cadet's uniform. However, the written examination was not so simple. At the time I was supposed to be suffering from German measles, but I never thought it was that which made me fail so ignominiously, though Bud came up to London with me and instructed me on what to eat for lunch, etc. Many of his instructions I followed in later examinations.

Bud was furious with the admirals, telling them that they had turned down the best candidate he had ever had. Furthermore, he did not send the usual school report when I left, but sent a letter to my father singing my praises. I think it was this evidence of appreciation that softened the blow for, somewhat surprisingly, I do not remember much disappointment. It must, nevertheless, have presented my father with a dilemma: what was he to do with this son of his? It had been assumed that I would get into Osborn (the naval college which trained naval officers) and my name had not been put down for any school should I fail. But as I came to know, he always seemed able to find a solution. He consulted a cousin who was chairman of the Fishmongers Company that sponsored a small but good public school in Norfolk and through his influence I was offered a place, provided I took the scholarship examination. That was arranged and I duly entered Greshams school the following autumn. In later years my housemaster told me that my performance in the examination was poor and he supposed that mathematics was my redeeming factor.

The first year at Greshams was crowned with success both in games and acting, while I did well enough at work to go up a class at the end of the year. My housemaster, who was retiring, wrote a glowing letter to my father about my prospects – I was not allowed to read it! My own memories of success were: 1) I passed the 'first class' swimming test, which had not been done in the first year before. 2) I had success at rugby football. In the first game I ever played I was put in the scrum, being rather a large boy, but then was removed to full back where I was on my own: a prestigious member of the school team came running towards me. Assuming he was on the way to score a try, I tackled him and brought him down – it seemed quite easy as I had been shown how to do that. Of course he might have been over-confident but the episode was repeated and that caused a sensation. I cannot remember how soon I played in the school team but it was not long afterwards. 3) I acted in the school play – an annual event taking place in an open-air theatre. I was chosen to play Viola in Shakespeare's *Twelfth Night*. I had difficulty in learning my part but did so with active help from other members of the cast – which I much appreciated – but in other respects I enjoyed the acting very much and a notice of the play in *The Times* picked out my performance for special praise. I always acted in the school play afterwards and in house plays as well, producing some of them. I believe a powerful element in my success was my mother's interest. When it was known I was to take part in *Twelfth Night* she arranged for a reading of the play to take place with the Rhys family, who were gifted with literary talents. My memory of those readings was the absorbing performance of the fool by Ernest Rhys, himself a writer, but best known as editor of the Everyman Library published by Dent. He enjoyed the part with such a rollicking enthusiasm.

7 HAMPSTEAD AND CATASTROPHE

After the war ended Hillcroft was sold and a house was bought which was a delight to live in: a Georgian building in Well Walk near Hampstead Heath. Its large windows and well-proportioned rooms were a joy and mother presided in the drawing-room with evident pleasure. Another delight was to look from one of the top rooms and see right across London to the Crystal Palace. My brother went to Cambridge to study natural science, winning a senior exhibition at Trinity College. My sister Thea became a Home Student at Oxford – she played lacrosse for the university – and I was doing well at Greshams. Everything seemed set fair except that when Thea was chosen to play in a trial match she was not selected to play for England. She was so angry that she never played lacrosse again!

In 1920 the family went for a holiday in Brittany, where I contracted earache – it was bad enough for me to be sent to bed. Mother was also unwell, probably with an attack of asthma, but she got up and came into my room in her dressing-gown – she was absolutely lovely and I lay there basking in her beauty. The next morning I learned that she was dead. From that point on the family fell to pieces. We were all shattered. Almost at once I had the sense of mother's presence, which my sister thought beautiful but I was not sure. Uncle Sydney came over from England to shepherd the family back home. I was sick on the boat, the first time I had ever been seasick and then became 'ill' enough not to return to school. Aunt Alice and Uncle Sydney looked after me in their house near Ashwell till I recovered. An incident during this period remains in my memory: the headmaster sent me a very kind and insightful letter for which I should have been grateful but it embarrassed me.

My illness was never diagnosed but I am rather sure I was depressed and dissociated. Outwardly I did not show much at school. I continued my achievements at games, playing in all the first teams for nearly all the time I was there and becoming captain of hockey. I continued to act and produce house plays but except for mathematics and, later, biology, my work performance deteriorated. It may be of interest to record, in view of the amount of writing and editing that I have done in later life, that my English was especially bad. On one occasion we were given, as homework, the task of writing a poem on climbing Mount Everest – mine was read out as by far the worst. On another occasion I wrote an essay on 'science and the classics' and I attacked classical education in a rough and rather stupid way. It was a bad, unbalanced essay and the English master, who also taught classics, spent the whole of a period lambasting it, writing across the top of my production 'What you want is a good classical education to improve your spelling'. I bore no resentment against either master, nor did I feel humiliated for I greatly admired both and shall never forget the classics master reading Hamlet's 'To be or not to be . . . '. He left me with a lasting appreciation of Shakespeare. I just knew their estimation of my work was correct, they had got it right. It made me experience my true – rather than my degraded – inner nature, which was the harbinger of my true self. My patchy work performance was, I learned from analysis, a symptom of a profound splitting. But on the surface, it was all very puzzling.

Apparently it was so to my teachers as well. The mathematics masters, and later the biology master, were my advocates although I once surprised the French master by coming top in the French examination at the end of term. A feature of his teaching was that he did not do much of it. He was a Frenchman and gave one a sense of the language, which was also talked sporadically by my parents. I had a natural mathematical ability and so mathematics was mostly easy and several times I became what I can only describe as inspired by some proposition or other – it was as though I knew about it without being taught and the mathematical logic came to take over and filled me with excited delight. In the end that experience frightened me and I gave up mathematics with some relief.

Foy, who taught biology, was no schoolmaster. He had disgraced himself by getting a third-class degree. He was a friend of Julian Huxley at Oxford and I can only hope that he found his way back into research where he belonged. He told me what to read and let me work in his private room, where I sometimes could not help listening to what went on in his classes: he simply could not keep order and would shout at one boy after another 'Go to the headmaster', so that there would be a trail of boys going along to Mr Eccles's study. I taught myself with his help and he wanted me to go for a scholarship at Trinity. He asked about my physics and chemistry and after that I heard no more of it. The truth of the matter, which I half knew, was that I could learn but was virtually unteachable. Nevertheless, I became a school hero largely on account of my other achievements. This I accepted as my right but it was all unreal and a kind of necessary deception. I think it was for this reason that I developed an intolerance of praise – the dispenser of it had been deceived!

But I was not entirely a copybook public schoolboy, and I practised open and concealed rebellion. Perhaps my lamentable efforts in writing English and my patchy academic record are examples of this. Writers featured in my development and my father wrote books, so I had good models to follow, but not at school! There was another area in which I disobeyed, though I think for rather more mature reasons. The 'honour system', as it was called, was special to Greshams school. When a boy entered the school he was asked to promise 'not to swear, not to smoke and not to say or do anything indecent'. Furthermore he was asked to inform his housemaster if he knew of any boy who failed to keep his promise. Smoking was no problem to me, as my parents had promised me £21 if I did not smoke till I became of age. I was not given to swearing much and only indecency presented something of a problem – I was not sure what the term covered. It was true that Bud had given warnings, not altogether clear, about homosexuality in public schools and it probably related to that, but when I became house captain I asked my housemaster for clarification and to my surprise he referred to masturbation. This I did not intend to give up since I thought it facilitated my performance in hockey.

Soon after I arrived at the school we were asked to write down what we thought of the 'honour system' and the headmaster complimented me on what I wrote. When I became head of house my views had, however, changed: moderate smoking would not be censured, a few swear words did not matter and I did not think inoffensive homosexuality was indecent. When W.H. Auden wrote me a love poem I was embarrassed but it did not seem to me indecent. None the less I made an investigation into homosexuality in the school and my friend the head boy was a fount of information. He told me of a boy in his house whom he had had to restrain from climbing out of the window because he wanted to get into the bed of a boy in my house and so relieve his lusts. The head boy did not consider it his duty to inform the housemaster. So I became increasingly critical of the 'honour system'. When I became house captain I secretly modified it so that I need do nothing about failures to comply with the letter of the promise. I do not think it was a good system and am glad to know that it is no longer in existence.

Other symptoms of rebellion: in the sixth form we were allowed to work in our studies, and on one occasion I went to sleep, waking up when I should have been in class. I hastily went there and said that I had been asleep, expressing regrets of course. The headmaster took a dim view of it and issued a public rebuke in the form of a speech about what I, as a school prefect, had done: 'Most regrettable' he called it, the most severe form of censure he could deliver. Another incident was this: at the end of my last term it was customary for the housemaster to deliver a homily on the retiring house captain. This he did, listing all my achievements, which I found embarrassing enough, and infuriating me by saying that in spite of all my activities I had passed all my examinations! I had taken it for granted that I would do that. I think that was the first time I had an intimation of my inability to tolerate public praise. In my speech of reply, I teased and ragged the housemaster in the worst of taste. I am still too ashamed of myself to remember what I said. Though I did not truly like him I owe much to him and Greshams.

All this does not sound like a catastrophe. Indeed from the outside it was a success story but I was split in two and gained little satisfaction from my achievements. The catastrophe was, however, much more apparent in my home life: it ceased to exist any more. Forty Well Walk became a house I could stay in, but no more than that. After a time my father married again, to a Russian, Vera Volkovski, but it did not work at all. I liked her and felt comfort in her presence but she had a 'nervous breakdown' and retired to a nursing home – I never forgave her for deserting me, for many years later when she wanted me to visit her, I found I could not do it. It was a bitter blow to my father, who departed to White Russia to reorganize agriculture there under the aegis of the Friends. My sister tried to keep a home going and I became closer to her than before: she introduced me to poetry and the Russian novelists and dramatists so I could participate in her literary interests. She also introduced me to John Galsworthy, who was fond of her. When we met he spent the time showing me photographs of his recent American tour – they bored me and the meeting was not a success. She also thought it would be nice for me to have a girlfriend and arranged for me to be invited by a Miss (probably Daphne) DuMaurier to accompany her to a concert in the Queens Hall. That was not a success either, because I just did not know how to relate to such a beautiful young woman and was embarrassed by the luxury of her home life. I had no money and did not know how to make a return for the generous treatment I received. I could not ask her to Well Walk, which had become a shambles.

I learned from Thea that she went to Bloomsbury group parties and I wanted to go to one of them, but she refused and hinted that what went on there was not suitable for one of such tender years as myself. Of course, I thought of orgies but in reality she probably went with David Garnett, who was fond of her and wanted to marry her. She probably thought I would be in the way as she was (I believed) his mistress by then and I later found out that he thought me a nuisance anyway. I was also introduced to a Miss Lillian Bowes Lyon and learned that her family was annoyed that George Windsor (later King George VI) was to marry into a junior branch of the family. Lillian Bowes Lyon was a poetess and lived in luxury; this did not embarrass me when Thea was there because she showed

Thea

no embarrassment at all. So I lived in my sister's glamorous shadow while Well Walk went down hill.

Eventually Thea departed to Paris, where she lived in a small hotel in the rue Monsieur le Prince towards the Seine end of the Boulevard St Michel in the Latin Quarter. For two or three holidays I went over to stay with her and browsed around the city. I liked it there and was introduced to French food and *cigarettes jaunes*, a particularly noxious, sulphurous type of indulgence. Although most of the time I was on my own, Thea and I had good times together. I particularly remember the theatre, though my French was not good enough to understand much of the script: this also applied to the opera, where we viewed a magnificent production of *Boris Godunov* from the gallery. I never found out what my sister did during the day, but I gleaned that she pursued her literary interests and knew people like Gertrude Stein and James Joyce, though that may be quite untrue – in any case, she never took me to make their acquaintance.

My father eventually returned from White Russia and was, I learned, in a bad way; I assume he was depressed. He went to see the neurologist Henry Head, who told him he should find something with which to occupy himself. He embarked on a campaign for the revival of agriculture. He wrote a book, *The Rebuilding of Rural England*, and a pamphlet in which he collaborated with Thea. He started lecturing round the country and founded The Rural Reconstruction Association. (He continued this work until his death at 85 in 1960.) He also wrote articles on the European peasantry and similar subjects. In addition he revived his knowledge of Greek by studying the New Testament in that language. In all this he had success: he became a fellow of the Historical Society and had the main substance of his political policies adopted by all three political parties. During this time he talked about the background of politics and of various devices he used to get his ideas across, all of which left me with a decidedly cynical view of how important matters were decided. It also gave me ideas which were useful later on when I engaged in the politics of psychological societies.

I admired and appreciated all that he was doing in the later part of his life and felt reasonably comfortable about his relative neglect of his children. I think we knew he was available if needed and with that thought we were all left to get on with our own lives in our own way; I doubt whether my brother would have agreed with my view, though my father helped him to start a highly successful career. Through his connections he gave Chris access to the Crown Estate Agents from which he obtained a position in Nottinghamshire, where he built up one of the largest land agencies in the country. He became a member of the establishment and inherited the family fortunes and property at Odsey.

During the remainder of the time at Well Walk, I was very much left to my own devices, with a good deal of help from various sources, especially women. Dr Stella Churchill was one of the women who were kind to me. She had met my father in my last term at Greshams. Her son was at the school and she had come down for the school play. Their relationship continued and they might have married, but I supposed she thought my father would be a bit of a handful. She provided parties at her house in Regent's Park and twice paid for a holiday, once skiing in Switzerland, when I was the nominal tutor to her son, and once in Brittany, where I made sexual approaches to a girl for the first time and greatly enjoyed the vivacity of a French barmaid – I knew then that I could feel attracted to girls and that I was attractive to them. I had the same experience on a holiday in Walberswick, to which my father and Stella Churchill came too. Help of a different kind came in the form of holidays in Donegal where the Franklin family owned a large house in which they held house parties. We went to them more than once because my brother was a friend of Cecil Franklin, the son of a successful bullion dealer.

8   CAMBRIDGE

Greshams had been a place with a firm framework and I half-dreamt my way through my success. School life began well, but after my mother's death and the disintegration of family life, it changed. I did not realize why at the time but I knew later that I had split and that my emotional life had gone underground so that much of the pleasure in achievements was lost and my self-esteem became precarious. I could not stand praise because of that – I simply thought I had deceived those who very often made a correct assessment. The teachers saw that something was wrong and suggested that I stay on for another year after I had planned to leave so that I could become house captain, which would give me a chance to mature. That was a helpful suggestion and was accepted.

As I did not know what I wanted to do with my life I accepted my brother's suggestion that, as I was good at biology, I might become a doctor. He thought it would be a good idea to have a member of that profession in the family. I am not clear whether he knew that some Fordhams thought it a disgrace to be ill and would only let the doctor in by the back door, and thereby expressed his ambivalence towards me, or whether this story reflects my own doubts about the profession. I suspect the latter.

I went up to Trinity College, Cambridge, when I was nineteen, having passed my first MB from school, and found that I could plunge into study in the way I liked, which was liberating. It was not only the subjects – zoology, comparative anatomy and physiology – that were congenial but the university atmosphere left me free enough to learn in the way I enjoyed. It was only human anatomy which I surveyed with foreboding: the mass of facts to be learned appalled me but I found a way round that, as I shall detail later. During the first two years I had two sets of examinations to pass (Part One of the Medical Sciences tripos and the second MB), so I worked quite hard, although I attended as few lectures as possible. Games fell into the background: I played rugger and hockey for Trinity and once was selected to play in the second university eleven for hockey. However, I was not paying enough attention to my health and physical fitness so my reflexes worked too slowly for the higher level of performance. I dropped cricket altogether.

During my first year I thought I was doing well enough to enter for the Senior Scholarship examination at Trinity and won an exhibition. This did much to mitigate my patchy intellectual performance at school – I had a brain and could use it. I wrote a rather impudent letter to the headmaster of Greshams, J.R. Eccles, telling him of my success, because I was sore at the school's doubts about whether I was intelligent or not (which I had learned about from a friend who visited the school as an old boy and occasionally attended masters' meetings).

When I contemplate my life at Trinity I recognize that I was something of an outsider: I did not seem to fit in anywhere properly, I never felt at home amongst the medical students and never engaged in their social life. The same applied to the rugger and hockey fraternities – I made no friends in either of these groups. My friends, if I knew what that meant, were nearly all my intellectual superiors in one way or another and they could not understand my athleticism. My main friend was Carew Meredith, who had a brilliant mind; and round him congregated a group of scholars, most of whom did not fulfil their promise. They were above me in intellectual ability and I struggled along behind them like that small boy of my earlier years, who could not keep up with his elder brother and sister. Carew Meredith was a mathematician and he won any prize that was going, but when it came to research his efforts were disappointing. However, he had wide-ranging intellectual interests and introduced me to *Ulysses* by James Joyce and *The Waste Land* by T.S. Eliot. He studied Wittgenstein's *Tractatus* with comprehension, which only a greatly admired Fellow called Ramsey could also do. I certainly could not. I enjoyed the philosophies of Bertrand Russell and George Berkeley. *Ulysses* I could only read with pleasure some years later but the mood of T.S. Eliot was strangely congenial. Carew was secretary of the Heretics Society, a meeting place for intellectuals. They met to hear distinguished speakers every so often; Carew's minutes were always short but left one gasping at the penetrating, sometimes witty and sometimes sardonic appraisals.

I tried other social groups, the Labour Club and the Musical Society, but did not seem to fit in well in either. I don't know that I was a much better fit amongst the 'county' set. Because I was a Fordham I was invited to large luxurious houses and to hunt balls. How I wished that I had enough money to ask some girl that I was fond of, rather than be the guest of some girl who fancied me! Another source of entertainment was with a group of undergraduates who were collected together by the wife of the professor of architecture. I don't know why she selected me as the recipient of her generosity, but it was very welcome.

The main emotional event of the first year was falling in love with a married woman. Her husband, Erskine Childers, was a contemporary of mine at Greshams and came up to Cambridge the same term. He lived out of college because he had married his beautiful and gifted wife. When he introduced me to her it was as his best friend. That surprised me because I did not think I knew him very well at school (I did not know anybody very well in those days). I fell in love with Ruth almost immediately with the kind of passionate possessive love which emerged from time to time with my mother. I went through all the illusions and delusions that such love evokes until I eventually recognized that she could not return my feelings and I became despairing, bitter and angry with her. She was consistently kind and tolerant until I became verbally offensive – I am grateful to her for the way she tried to help me in my dilemma, even though I became very angry. We did not meet for months after that and when we did all my passion had evaporated. I would have liked to go on knowing her but at the time I had no heart for it.

That love did much to open up and develop my relations with other women; none satisfactory and some were quite dangerous, others were trivial. There were two more serious relationships which fortunately did not last, for I was in no position to marry either of the women, and that was what they were after. I became engaged to one of the women, a young South African. She was, I think, rather bewildered by it all. Eventually her mother came over to England and arranged a party, to which my father was invited. He was seated next to a supposedly aristocratic friend – my father was not impressed and told me that this woman was in the process of divorce and was amusing herself with the *demi-monde* until the divorce was over! Eventually it came to buying an engagement ring and I took my fiancée to The Artificers Guild, the shop in which my father had once had an interest. They had some beautiful stones that could be made into a ring by one of their craftsmen. Her mother was furious: nothing but a diamond would do for her daughter, and that I did not like and could not afford anyway. She carried her off to South Africa, so that was the end of that – I think we were both relieved.

My other love affair of any consequence was with a lively and responsive French girl and we had good times together. I could not leave it at that but had to go on to propose marriage, which was hopelessly unrealistic, especially as she told me that her mother had already arranged her marriage! When she returned to France I went over to Paris to meet her parents. The meeting was not a success and she was forbidden to see me. We corresponded, however, and had a clandestine meeting in the gardens at Versailles. That was the end – when I arrived home a letter came from her mother to say that her daughter would have no more to do with me. I was very hurt and showed it to my father, who said he knew how to reply to such a woman and he took over. But I was quite shattered and developed violent headaches. My father, to my astonishment, removed these by passing his hand over my forehead. He told me he had 'healing powers' and that he used them with my mother. He did not like doing it. I mention these incidents more to illustrate my father's helpfulness and knowledge of the world than to display my erotic innocence and blindness.

Returning to work, I dealt with my anxieties about anatomy by going, during the long vacation in the summer, to Edinburgh where there was a course given at Surgeons' Hall by J. Ryland Whitaker. It appeared that I was not the only one who wanted what amounted to a cram course in anatomy, indeed, the students were mostly from Oxford and Cambridge. Whitaker was a brilliant teacher and one of the few from whom I could learn. I attended the course twice and passed the anatomy paper of the second MB almost entirely on what I learned from him. I cherish the copy of his *Anatomy of the Nervous System* which he gave me and I bought a copy of *Outlines of Human Osteology* by F.O. Ward, from which he would quote. It is a small volume and on the title page is a quotation: 'True brevity consists, not in expressing ideas in a *short space* but conveying them in a *short time*'.

At the end of my second year at Cambridge I took the second MB and gained a second-class degree in the first part of the Natural Sciences tripos. I was disappointed but I thought it forgivable since many students took three years over it, whilst I had taken two and had my medical studies in addition. In my third year I studied physiology only for the second part of the tripos and enjoyed that wholeheartedly; I did not work so hard and enjoyed myself more socially. I did not get first-class honours as I had hoped and that put a stop to any opportunity to engage in research, which I had half aspired to. Under the surface I was angry but I only knew that later. At the time I thought it was due to my inability to learn subjects that did not engage my interest. Consequently in an examination some of my answers were less than adequate.

What did I think were the advantages of going to an old university, besides the acquisition of knowledge and having a degree that would help in later life? My own feelings were that the tradition was grafted on to that of my family and was thus a support. But in addition there was the opportunity to meet men with first-class minds and personalities. They gave one a sort of measuring rod for future assessment, not only of myself but also of others. There were two men of this kind who most impressed me: one was Adrian, subsequently Lord Adrian, who pioneered the study of nerve functioning; the other was Gowland Hopkins, the discoverer of vitamins and the founder of biochemistry, at least in Cambridge. Adrian was my tutor but what impressed me most were his research papers: they were short, beautifully clear and always contained discoveries that were absolutely secure. Hopkins I admired for other reasons; he was not a popular teacher and except for his research seminars, his classes were poorly attended, but I found what he said, in his rather halting manner, invariably inspiring. Another feature of Trinity, and probably other colleges as well, was that some of the Fellows would ask undergraduates to dine with them and this made a bridge between students and teachers. These meetings were nearly always very enjoyable. This aspect of social life in the university seems to have lapsed, which is a pity.

Where had I got to at Cambridge? I think I could say nowhere. I had discovered that I did not really want to be a doctor, or rather had begun to realize that. Nor do I really think research would have suited me. My emotional life was maturing but it was liable to become frustrated and chaotic. I think much good had come from divesting myself of some of the false trappings of my previous successes at school.

9 ST BARTHOLOMEW'S HOSPITAL

I moved to London when I was twenty-two, a mildly disappointed man. I had not achieved a first in the tripos, nor did I think I deserved it, so my aspirations to do research had been frustrated; I thought I was falling back on being a doctor. None the less I entered for the Schuter scholarship in anatomy and physiology at St Bartholomew's Hospital. When I looked at the physiology paper there was a question on inhibition, a subject which had engaged my interest so I knew quite a lot about it, indeed up to research standards. I thought to myself: 'This is a scholarship paper and there is everything to gain if I do well and nothing to lose, since I have already been accepted as a student at the hospital.' So I took a risk and spent as much time as I wanted on the first question and less on the second, which was also quite interesting. That left two questions unanswered so I wrote some notes on these and left it at that. I went on to the practical part of the examination, in which we were asked to do a simple titration. Whilst starting on this, to my surprise the examiners arrived. They told me they had been impressed with my answers in the written work: the first was brilliant and the second not far behind; they proposed to give me the mark of 98 per cent and would have given 100 per cent had they been allowed to. I was astounded and let all the fluid run out of the pipette – they said it did not matter, anybody could do that! I think these two physicians were puzzled by my subsequent rather indifferent performance, but there were so many facts to learn in an unintelligent way and I have always thought that too many facts obstructed my thinking. My work as a student was good enough, however, for the Professor of Medicine to invite me to become his house physician on the Unit provided I passed my MB in the summer – I failed and that ended any ambition to further the cause of scientific medicine. I eventually joined the 'firm' under Dr Raymond Chandler, a pioneering chest physician, and Dr Hinds Howell, a gifted neurologist. I believe the appointment suited me better than the Unit, since I was given more responsibility because the consultants were not there all the time, whereas the professor would have been.

The Well Walk house had been sold and so I lived for a time in the house of Mrs Corbett Fisher, who was a very agreeable friend of the family. My father soon started building a small house for himself just outside the Quaker village of Jordans in Buckingham-shire, and he lived in the Quaker hostel while the house was being constructed. Eventually, after the episode with the French girl, my father introduced me to a woman, Molly Swabey, who would contain my sexuality and who was a more suitable personality. Molly was both intelligent and attractive, and in 1928, after a short time, we married. A measure of stability was introduced into my life. I was still a student at the time and short of money, but Molly wanted to work so as to build up a career for herself.

Molly was the daughter of a country parson and was obsessed with what she called the degeneration of his life with his large imposing wife. I could not agree with her assessment and I liked her father. Her views extended to other relatives but they also seemed agreeable people. Be that as it may, Molly was determined not to be like them. She had lived in Paris, for how long I never knew, and when she came back she lived in London and edited the journal of a society which promoted adult education. That was to prove a jumping-off point for becoming a journalist.

Together we had just enough to live on. We rented a small flat in Bloomsbury, later moving to another small flat in Boundary Road, St Johns Wood, where we stayed until after I was qualified and finished the job as house physician at Bart's. Later we took a one-room garden flat whilst I worked for a higher examination, which, if passed, would make me a member of the Royal College of Physicians – a necessary qualification if I were to become a consultant physician. It was a somewhat hand-to-mouth existence but very much worthwhile for both of us.

Soon after I left Cambridge Carew Meredith abandoned university life to live near us in Bloomsbury, collecting a number of interesting friends around him, thus making a small community which we joined. He undertook a psychoanalysis and married at the end of it; he must have been a difficult and challenging patient. The other person I could call a friend during this period was Alan Maberley, also a doctor, but intending to become a psychotherapist. He was a somewhat uncouth-looking man who had married a very beautiful woman – his friendship became important later on.

During this time I became more interested in medicine, especially neurology. Hinds Howell had developed a treatment for trigeminal neuralgia, a very painful condition. He was skilful at injecting the Gasserian ganglion at the base of the brain with alcohol and thus killing the fifth nerve which was causing the trouble. He asked me to do a follow-up of his cases, which I did, and he published the results with a pleasing reference to my work. I also wrote my MB thesis on the influence of the central nervous system on the blood vessels of the skin. That was my first experience of making a discovery contrary to current knowledge: my results showed that responses of the blood vessels were influenced by lesions in the spinal cord and perhaps higher centres in the nervous system as well, whereas previous work had studied only peripheral influences. My findings filled me with misgivings. I repeated the experiments over and over again and could not feel convinced until I had photographed the result. Nor could I feel safe until I had developed a theory that would account for the evidence. When I presented this work to the examiners, the professor at Cambridge suggested I should publish the paper in *The Journal of Physiology*; I did not do so, thinking, in my arrogance, that the professor was wrong, it was nothing like good enough. Yet to have done so would have furthered my idea of becoming a neurologist.

There was another piece of original work that I did on my own initiative whilst still a house physician. A number of cases of sub-arachnoid haemorrhage came onto the ward and a treatment for it was to reduce the intracranial pressure by drawing off some of the cerebrospinal fluid. I did that in each case adding concurrently a measurement of the blood pressure. The CSF pressure went down and the blood pressure rose, suggesting a danger of renewed haemorrhage into the brain and so further endangering life. The prognosis in these cases was not good but I got the impression that they none the less appeared in the post-mortem room too frequently, though no questions were asked. I published the evidence suggesting that the treatment might be dangerous. Hinds Howell knew about all this, and perhaps my enterprise made him think well enough of my work to encourage me to apply for the post of house physician at the National Hospital for Nervous Diseases, the most sought-after position for a prospective neurologist to hold. He encouraged me even though I did not have the membership degree of the Royal College of Physicians, generally held to be a necessary prerequisite for successful application. He apparently supported me so strongly that his colleagues reproached him for his excessive zeal.

In retrospect I believe it was fortunate that I was not able to pursue my interest, although there were good prospects had I done so. Had I been able to wait and apply again to the National Hospital it would have opened the way to becoming a neurologist on the staff at St Bartholomew's, where there was likely to be a vacancy. Fortunately or unfortunately I could not wait: I had no money left and even then the salary of a house physician was much too low, and the post would have taken me away from Molly for far too long. I think the outcome was for the best, for I think that to have become a neurologist would have mobilized my inhumanity. At that time there was little therapeutic work that could be done and it was the fascination of tracking down the location of lesions, combined with studying how the brain worked, that fascinated me – people hardly mattered.

Whilst I was a student and house physician, my interest in psychoanalysis trailed behind medicine but was not entirely forgotten, and on one occasion it was ridiculed by Chandler. There was a neurotic patient in one of the beds and he told me to put a screen round her bed and 'psychoanalyse her'! I had a slight interest in psychiatry – I believe that I was the only student to attend Porter Phillips' out-patient clinic on one occasion. This was because I had half-consciously been intrigued by Phillips' capacity to empathize with his psychotic patients. I had noticed this when attending sessions at Bethlem Hospital. He did not say much, just enough to get the patients to display their delusions or other psychopathology. In the out-patient department at Bart's he likewise said very little – he just looked at his patients benignly and I felt the patients loved him. However, there was an interest in patients' emotions from time to time. There was a male patient who had undergone a supposedly successful abdominal operation: when his surgeon came to visit him and sat down beside his bed, the patient announced with considerable emotion that he was going to die. The surgeon was visibly alarmed and told the patient that he was not to talk like that! The patient died.

In considering my life as a medical student and medical practitioner I recognize how traumatic much of it was. It introduced me to life in the raw: the constant contact with human beings in pain and distress, combined with one's frequent incapacity to help much, led to a defensive depersonalization and inflation (playing the doctor-god with power over life and death). My good fortune was to work for good physicians and on a ward where there was a remarkable sister – Sister Hope. She kept her house physicians on a leash and for a number of diseases (pneumonia, heart failure, and rheumatic fever being the most important) I had to prescribe a number of drugs which she would use in her nursing of patients. She did not prevent me from having ideas of my own within her own requirements and so I learned much about medical treatments from her. I got on well with her – what happened to the house physicians who did not I cannot imagine. In a sense she was in charge of the therapeutic work on her ward and it engaged my admiration. She was no respecter of persons and was full of scathing anecdotes and comments on members of the medical profession. On one occasion she told me of an unusually interesting case which a number of consultant physicians were invited to examine. They were all assembled discussing the symptoms and making tests until Sister Hope noticed that the patient was dead and drew their attention to that fact! They all traipsed out with their tails between their legs.

Nor did she spare me: when I asked her what she thought was

happening to the sub-arachnoid patients she replied: 'What, do you mean to say you did not know you were killing them?' I was glad that I had no proof and that none of my senior physicians had called my actions into question. I stopped my research at once, however, for she was not only a good nurse but a discerning observer. But she was not always so scathing and would help me if I made a mistake. On one occasion towards the end of a 'duty' when I was on call for 24 hours for several days, I was tired. A patient came in who was ill enough to be admitted. I thought he had pneumonia and listening to the base of his lungs gave some confirmation of my guess. Now a pneumonia patient was nursed lying down, so I was surprised to find him sitting up when I arrived on the ward and Sister told me I had better examine him again because he had a typical history of heart failure. She was correct – besides being a good nurse she was also a clinician of considerable ability and I am convinced that today she would have trained as a doctor and risen high in that profession.

She was intensely loyal, except on one occasion. There was a patient who had intestinal symptoms and was extremely debilitated. I examined him several times carefully and could find nothing, becoming convinced that there was nothing there. Sister Hope went over my head to my superior and a surgeon was called in to perform an exploratory laparotomy. The patient died but my conclusion that there was no lesion in his abdomen was confirmed at the post-mortem. I was so furious with her that I got her up in the middle of the night simply to perform a blood transfusion on another patient, which she did in record time using an apparatus which she herself had invented! However, we became quite close friends and I was asked out to her favourite Chinese restaurant, once alone and once with Molly.

Later I was able to experience her nursing first hand. When Molly and I were living in Surrey, I contracted a fever and the general practitioner examined me, describing the symptoms of typhoid fever without apparently making that diagnosis. I had thought that if I was ever to need nursing I would somehow get myself into Hope ward, which I did and I then knew subjectively that what I had thought about her nursing was correct.

There was one other fact that I learned from Sister Hope. The mortality rate from pneumonia was lower on her ward than on any other. I asked her about it and she said that she herself had once had pneumonia and knew that it made all the difference whether a nurse stroked the skin with a damp cloth in one direction only, that is, towards the heart during the crisis. I had noticed that she sat like a lynx over her pneumonia patients when that crisis was on. Sister Hope died of a cerebral tumour almost immediately after retiring.

After taking the Membership examination money had almost run out and somehow I had to earn some. I took a locum in general practice, more to see what it was like than anything else, and went to see a general practitioner about joining him. I concluded that I was not qualified for the job and would need to take house jobs in surgery and obstetrics before I felt able to embark on that most difficult branch of the medical profession. Shortly after this Molly and I then went to a party and there we met a member of the London County Council who was influential in the Mental Hospital service. He told me that there was an appointment being advertised for a junior 'officer' at Long Grove Mental Hospital in Epsom. I applied and interviewed well, giving an account of my interest in the nervous system and mental disorders. I got the post, to the fury of the other applicants who had all had previous experience in psychiatry. That appointment led indirectly to my becoming a psychotherapist and eventually a Jungian analyst.

10 PSYCHIATRY, CHILD GUIDANCE, ANALYSIS

Now we had an income, Molly and I found a bungalow, though it was more like a shack, near Epsom on the edge of Down country and I started on my new appointment, wondering how I should fare; Molly continued working in London. I still kept contact with St Bartholomew's by working in Hinds Howell's neurological clinic where another neurologist, Dr Carmichael, also attended. That I enjoyed. Work in the mental hospital was less enjoyable, especially as I started off in the chronic wards – where I could not do much harm, I suppose. I found the smell of paraldehyde in the old patients' ward especially repulsive and the monotonous routine of signing certificates and prescriptions did not provide any time for getting to know patients. Indeed, the nurses were surprised and a bit irritated if I wanted to see any of the patients alone for more than a few minutes.

The best event of this period was the birth in 1933 of our son Max, who was a great joy to both of us, except when he woke us up at night, as such a vigorous infant would do. Molly was more tolerant but I could not bear his crying. After his birth Molly was left alone with Max for most of the day. She did not like that and became restless, as I did too but for different reasons.

Very little work was required of a medical officer in the so-called mental hospital: there was a conference with the superintendent in the morning; after that one went on ward rounds, which meant little more than signing certificates and repeat prescriptions – the rest of the day was then virtually free. Mainly to fill in the time I started to insist on spending time with patients and found that productive: I learned quite a lot by doing so, though there was nobody with whom I could discuss my findings in any detail. One of the patients was 'The devil's disciple', whom I saw at regular interviews and with whom I began to recognize the outlines of a scapegoat myth. I do not remember the details but he was tormented by evil influences which he thought would rot away his internal organs, making death imminent – when that happened he would be able to take away the sins of humanity.

At the time I had been persuaded by Alan Maberley to read Jung. I had considerable contempt for Jung's work at the time, but I had grasped his ideas about archetypes and the collective unconscious. Studying that patient made me think, to give the devil his due, that if Jung was talking sense I could look up the subject of scapegoats in Frazer's *The Golden Bough* and find there analogies between the rituals and myths of primitive man. Many of the themes the patient displayed in his delusions were there – they were not identical but the pattern of them was unmistakable. That was the first time I could make any sense of Jung. I was much more interested in Freud and tried to use his technique as I imagined it to be. I therefore tried seeing another patient regularly. I placed him on the medical couch and tried to get him to free associate, without much success – nor did my crude interpretations meet with much response. He suffered from persecution by electrical influences and tried to get information about the electrical effects of one person on another, so I lent him my copy of Bayliss's *Textbook of Physiology*, which contained information about the electrical component in nervous actions, from which he made copious notes. The patient had been given a poor prognosis and it was thought that he would never leave hospital. He improved so much, however, that the nurses asked me what I was doing. I tried to explain to them but they remained bewildered – for that matter, so did I. I did not know whether it was my attempt at psychoanalysis or the work he did with the book on physiology, or neither, that had facilitated sufficient recovery for him to be discharged.

Both cases provided food for thought, though I could not then do much more than be puzzled. At that time, it was widely thought that psychotic patients did not develop a transference. Case One seemed to do so, for he installed me as a helper in his suffering. Case Two did not develop anything like that but his recovery had some characteristics of a transference cure. Then there was the idea that psychotic delusions contained a 'normal' element, as the first case seemed to demonstrate, for the delusions had characteristics which Jung called archetypal, including myth-like configurations.

There was another case I remember particularly. A female patient, who was in a sub-acute ward, became disturbed and the nurses wanted me to move her to an acute ward. I asked about her dreams and she told me of very dramatic archetypal ones of devils dragging her down to hell. I wanted to see whether it was possible to avoid these dreams being acted out, which it seemed to me the staff wanted almost to induce by moving her. So I talked to her about the dreams and refused to transfer her to an acute ward. The next I heard was that the transfer had taken place over my head. So I was left with the theoretical quandary that a psychotic was not supposed to have an unconscious. According to archetype theory at that time, ego consciousness could be replaced by archetypal consciousness in the psychoses and I assumed that meant that archetypal dreams would not occur. Yet here was a psychotic patient having archetypal dreams which were supposed to compensate the ego. So I tried to find and support the ego, although without success.

My enquiring mind would not leave me alone but it kept coming up against obstructions in a hospital which was run in a quasi-military and custodial way. Besides the three senior medical officers, who agreed to this functioning of the institution, there were four of us who wanted to reflect and do what we could to change things. We wanted to understand our patients better and do what we could to modify the accepted procedures. We could not do much and it had to be clandestine. Sometimes, however, one of us, especially a Dr Walk, who subsequently became a superintendent and a much respected psychiatrist, would do things of which the superintendent disapproved and he would be reprimanded at the staff meetings that were held every morning. I did not find much response to my analytic thinking – I suppose it was too abstract.

At this time I was becoming more and more interested in

psychodynamic ideas and this was increased by a renewed meeting with Godwin Baynes, who had known my family at Limpsfield many years back. Molly and I were on a walking holiday in the Black Forest and that had brought us near Switzerland. Accordingly we walked on to Zurich where I knew Baynes was living, working as Jung's assistant. I contacted him and he, to my delight, remembered who I was, so he took Molly and me out to a prolonged lunch. Soon after that he came back to England, where we maintained contact and I learned that there was a small group of Jungians, centring on the Analytical Psychology Club, in London.

As time went on both Molly and I became more and more restless. I began to hate the hospital spirit and its routines, viewing the prospect of continuing as a medical officer with dismay. In addition, Molly hated the isolation of her life – it is true that she had Max, but that was not enough. The weekends were better, with friends visiting us; they were sometimes enlivened by cricket. I played for a team collected by Desmond Flower, a director of Cassell's publishing house. One day in 1934 Alan Maberley, knowing of my dislike of the hospital work, told me that there was a vacancy for a Fellowship in Child Psychiatry at the London Child Guidance Clinic, an enterprise sponsored by the Commonwealth Foundation in New York. It would mean a drop in my salary if I won the post and it only lasted for one year, but Molly was keen for me to apply and said that she would work to supplement our income. Before applying I asked Baynes whether he would analyse me, even though I had little money. His reply was favourable and I applied for and won the Fellowship. It was a daring move, especially as I had little medical knowledge of children and no special liking for them except for Max, to whom I was devoted although anxious about my capacity to look after him properly.

So we moved up to London and found a basement flat in Tavistock Square quite close to a shop where Molly started work. It sold attractive children's toys and was near enough to the flat for Molly to be easily available if needed by the childminder. It was not ideal and I feared Max would suffer – perhaps he did. He screamed enormously if his needs were not being met and then Molly would come rushing back from her shop. Max was a vigorous infant who made his needs abundantly clear, so because of his help we were not such inadequate parents as it might seem. There was, however, one near-disaster which haunted me over the years. Max went off his food and I tried to force him to take his bottle, which made matters much worse. I consulted Baynes, who was analysing me, and also a paediatrician, Dr Franklin, whom I had known at Bart's. They both arrived at our flat at the same time, Franklin with boxes of baby foods to try out, Baynes with all his psychic tentacles working at top speed. It was he who took over; he announced that his wife had been trained in Truby King methods and Max should be sent to a special Truby King home for infants that she knew of. That was done and Molly soon went to see him there. She found that they had isolated him in a cot away from other babies: she just picked him up, took him home and rapidly nursed him back to his own self. That incident shows Molly at her best: instinctive and decisive. I feel deeply grateful to her for being like that, basically a good mother, as well as a great support to me in my unstable searching for a career to which I could devote myself. It sounds as if the marriage was one-sided – it was not, for I was also able to support her in her career as a journalist. This took off later when she joined the staff of *Vogue*, and organized a feature called 'Shop Hound'.

I found the work at the clinic interesting and enjoyable. As I was now beginning to think of myself as a Jungian, since I was being analysed by Baynes, I approached my work with the idea that the neurotic children, or those with behaviour disorders or even pre-psychotic children, were in trouble because of the unconscious conflicts of their parents, which was the Jungian position at the time. From that position one would expect the parents to be the main focus of the psychiatrist's attention. The psychiatrist was the leader of a team composed of himself, a psychologist and a psychiatric social worker, but they were expected to focus on the child and not the parents. The parents were seen only by the social worker. I had, therefore, to learn how to treat children, since I was expected to do so. In this procedure instruction was given by a supervisor. Mine was Dr Posthuma, a woman with a very subtle understanding of children, some of which she helpfully conveyed to me. Her technique was called the 'passive technique', so I did very little with the children and did not need to violate my Jungian orientation. To my surprise they tended to recover and though the psychiatric social workers saw the mothers regularly, they did nothing like analysing unconscious motives, as was required according to Jung's conceptions.

These observations, especially the capacity of children to get well though nothing much was done, made me question Jungian doctrine and I started to apply some features of my own analysis. I enquired about the children's dreams and encouraged them to paint or draw pictures. From these I learned some important facts. Archetypal images could be found in them, which was theoretically in line with Jungian thinking, but it was held that the archetypes were dangerous – they came from an unconscious out of which the child needed to separate himself. Accordingly I should not have expressed my interest to the children, nor encouraged them to paint and dream more. However, I was encouraged by another observation: children took pleasure and delight in fairy tales. What was significant was how therapeutic the active expression of the fantasies and my positive interest in them seemed to be. It was, I believe, because of this work that I gained a reputation for being able to treat severely disturbed children. All the same I still tended to enquire from psychiatric social workers whether they could not do more with a mother when I was at a loss with some child. I think that ended when Miss Lowden, the social worker that I particularly trusted and liked working with, told me bluntly that the mother of an autistic child I was treating was doing very well and I should get on with my work with the child, which was bearing fruit.

In order to test my Jungian colleagues, I demonstrated that child's pictures, which contained rebirth symbolism, at the Analytical Psychology Club. All its members could do was to enquire about the terrible state of the mother's unconscious. Much later on, after the end of the war, I also demonstrated the case in Zurich but nobody seemed interested except Mrs Jung, who became my ally. She went so far as to tell me about an archetypal dream of her grandchild. She also encouraged Dora Kalff, a patient of hers who was interested in Margaret Lowenfeld's sand play techniques, and introduced her to me.

After the Second World War had ended I had access to Jung's seminar on children's dreams. To my astonishment and pleasure he found archetypal images in them and even a symbol of the self, although he was never in favour of child analysis. My intense intellectual and personal conflict, which was endangering my Jungian position, possibly leading to isolation, was drawing to a close. Another incident further diminished my anxiety. When in New York I discussed a rich archetypal dream of a child at the Analytical Psychology Club, the home of anti-child analysis. To my surprise there was an interested audience and a well-informed discussion. Following it Frances Wickes, an analytical psychologist, invited me to her home to tell me that as a child she had dreamt a very rich and vivid archetypal dream, which she related to me. In her book *The Inner World of Childhood* she had warned of the danger these dreams presented to children, because to pay attention to them would push the child back into the unconscious. I assume that it was because she had discovered the untruth of her belief that she told me her dream, which evidently had been a source of inspiration, for it was beautiful and there was no danger in it. Later still Jung reported his own dream of the underground phallus in his *Memories, Dreams, Reflections*, commenting on it in glowing terms, so I was completely vindicated in my discoveries.

So much for aspects of my long struggle to interest Jungians in child psychology. I will now return to my work at the Child Guidance Clinic before the war, where a further revolution was taking place in my mind. I had no means of conveying what I knew to children themselves for Jung's method would mean amplifying their material with ethnological examples and this did not seem desirable. I do not know why I felt this; perhaps it was a relic of Mrs Wickes's caveat, for my student Lawrey Hawkey tried it once, building on a child's fascination with fairy tales. No very disastrous consequences followed, although the child became excited.

I found Melanie Klein's work much more important. I read *The Psychoanalysis of Children* with amazement and emotional shock. What she described made sense of much of my material, although not the more dramatic archetypal dreams and pictures, which I find puzzling even today because I am not convinced by Jung's explanation. Be that as it may, I applied as much of Klein as I could digest and found that my relation to children improved, sometimes quite dramatically. What impressed me with Klein's work? First of all her daring in listening to, and taking seriously, what children said and her use of play as a means of communication. Then there was her acute perception as to the meaning of their activities in relation to herself. There was also her understanding of children's fantasies as basic in their development, which was a contention of Jung's, found particularly in his *Psychology of the Unconscious*. More specifically, I discovered analogies between what Jung found in myths and what Klein found in small children's fantasies about their mothers' bodies. Most impressive of all was the way in which she interpreted unconscious processes in the child in terms which were appropriate to childhood. She was also very clear that children developed a transference. In this early period of my development I was becoming increasingly impressed with the importance of transference and critical of my analysts' handling of it in my own case and in others. I had found that children formed one and I thought Klein was correct.

During this period before the war my private life became complicated by a young woman who fell in love with me. This was related to playing cricket. I had gone on playing until, to my great satisfaction, I scored a century. I had never done that though I had, as a bowler, taken ten wickets more than once. On this occasion a large man was bowling slow off-breaks. He sent down a ball short of a length and I determined to sweep him to leg. The ball ricocheted off the top of my bat into my face and I was covered with blood – 100 not out, I was something of a hero again both in my own estimation and in that of others. Having scored a century I retired hurt.

After these cricket matches there would be parties and at one of them, Julia, an artist and a particularly beautiful woman, claimed that she had fallen in love with me. I did not resist her advances and she became my mistress. I was then involved with two women, which made my marriage complicated but I was determined to sustain it. Molly was tolerant when she found out and did not want a divorce. She was building up her career as a journalist and was, I believed, more interested in that than in me. My analysis with Baynes was under way at this time and Baynes certainly supported my extra-marital relationship with a woman. He conceived it as my making a relation with my anima, the female side of myself, and he thought that was important. He even compared it with Jung, who also developed a relation with a woman outside his marriage when he 'confronted the unconscious' and became unstable. I think this was true of me but his support contributed to the undermining of my marriage, which was unfortunate and a fault in his treatment of me.

After some months' work with Baynes he suggested that I go out to Zurich to meet Jung, with the object of training in Zurich. So I wrote to Jung telling him about Baynes's proposal and explaining that I should have to earn my living in Switzerland as I had no financial reserves at all. I received a favourable reply and I took out the last of my money in the bank to pay for the journey and my hotel expenses. On the way out I travelled with a young Jew, from whom I learned of the threat to his race that the Nazi movement presented (Hitler had not then seized power). He was seeking asylum in another country since he feared for his life. He described vividly the ruthless violence being directed at the Jews, especially by the Nazi Youth.

When I entered Jung's study I mentioned this event to start off the conversation, or so I thought. It was almost fatal to my project. Jung launched into a long dissertation on the whole subject of the Jews in relation to the Nazi movement. I listened with astonishment to the uninterrupted flow of interesting and often provocative ideas, thinking to myself that it was like my father when he was possessed by his much-loved conceptions. So just as I had learned that to interrupt my father was of no avail, I sat there listening to Jung. The interview was drawing to a close and he had paid no attention to my letter. Eventually I interrupted him: 'Oh no,' he said, 'you could not earn money out here, the country is invaded by refugees and only recently I have had the police after one of my foreign colleagues.' He trundled out, after inviting me to a seminar he was giving on the following morning. I went to that and was fascinated by its vitality, its erudition and the vivid way he responded to questions and comments. Following the seminar there was tea and I was delighted when he singled me out for attention and talked in a pleasing and human way.

Jung puzzled me. In my interview he had seemed quite inhuman, a strong contrast to the way he was in the seminar and in the

C. G. Jung

subsequent meeting over tea. I could not make head or tail of it all. I had heard that sometimes in his interviews Jung would speak indirectly to the patient's unconscious but, as with Baynes, I could do nothing but listen with respectful scepticism. I knew enough about theory to know that he was talking to the collective unconscious, but could he not have taken the occasion to wake up an Englishman to the impending horrors? I remained bemused. As I went back to England I became very angry – how could he drag me out to Zurich when he knew that my proposition was impossible; he must be seriously out of touch with human requirements or feelings! I was to come across that again later. I now know that I was relating to Jung with my anima, which had fallen in love with him. That is why I had a strong feeling of intimacy with him, like that which I had with my father but more tinged with Eros. To this was added a strong loyalty, which did much to prevent me from developing a closer relation with psychoanalysts.

I returned to work with Baynes. I call it work because only some of it was what might be called analysis: for instance, when he analysed my dreams, asking for associations and interpreting their meaning. Besides this there was much instruction and I was to read books, especially on anthropology, and was told stories, often about Jung and Baynes. After a time I was allowed to read Jung's seminars on dreams and visions, which I found particularly inspiring. Further, as Baynes was writing a book about me, he would read out long parts of it, with amplifications from alchemy, yoga and other sources. I believed this was in line with Jungian practice at the time. It was intended to help me assimilate the archetypal material from the collective unconscious which I was producing. I was also given instructions on what to do:

1) I had a lot of sexual fantasies about odd women whom I did not know. Baynes thought that was due to my inadequate sexual experience and suggested I should investigate prostitutes, which I did but without much benefit and I desisted. He supported his proposal by telling me that Jung always tested out his fantasies whenever possible – I did not think he understood the nature of my fantasies but citing Jung overcame my objections.

2) Towards the end of my first period of work with him, Baynes suggested that before starting as an 'analyst' I should get more experience in general practice. I do not know quite why he suggested this, unless he thought I should get wider experience of human beings and I think I did get some good and interesting clinical experience. Molly, Max and I departed to Barking for about one year, where I gained a great respect for bus drivers, many of whom lived there. They were a fine lot of men, who tended to get gastric ulcers.

I could perform the ordinary medical routines well, except that I had difficulty in remembering the names of patients and they did not like that. My senior partner was keen on obstetrics, so my anxieties about that only cropped up on one occasion when he was away. I disliked being called out to deal with the aftermath of miscarriages or abortions, I never knew which. I could do nothing but send the women to hospital afterwards, and the ruthless attitude of at least one woman I found horrifying. I was also reproached for being officious on one occasion. I discovered an advanced cancer of the rectum which had been missed before and sent the man to hospital, where he underwent the usual operations. The family reproached me with 'Why could you not have let him die without causing all that trouble'! I remember another incident: we ran a small dispensary with a few useful drugs in it. On one occasion we ran out of them all except for a cough mixture, which had some gastric irritants and a trace of morphia in it. I dealt out this mixture, diluted considerably in the cases with gastric symptoms. To my astonishment several patients, including those with intestinal symptoms, hailed it with enthusiasm and wanted more of it. It was an example of what is now called the placebo effect, for in no case could the medicine have had the supposed effect. Perhaps the trace of morphia accounted for it, but I doubt it, since I had diluted it far too much.

One more event struck me forcibly – it had psychiatric importance to me and indirectly supported the views of Jung on psychotic phenomena. I was called in to see a mother who was creating a disturbance, shouting out and yelling. I went into the house and asked the family to wait outside, which they did. I listened to her and gained the impression that she was hallucinating and that the voices were accusing her of having seduced her son sexually. I told her of my suspicion and she called in the family, accusing me of making slanderous suggestions. The son assumed a threatening attitude but I calmed them down by saying they knew she was mad and mad people sometimes had such ideas, which were quite untrue. They understood this. When they had retired again I found to my surprise that I was confronted by a calm and apparently normal person, who told me that what I said was quite true but the voices would go on accusing her. That was the first time I realized how easy it could be to form a rapport with an adult in an acute psychotic episode.

I will now return to my 'analysis'. As I have said, most of it could not be called analysis as I knew about it from reading Freud's papers on what he did. No attention was paid to the transference. I went at first three times a week and wrote down my lengthy dreams in a book. Baynes discoursed on them at considerable length and sometimes analysed them. Then there came a point where I went into a sort of trance and Baynes told me that a good way to catch my fantasies was to try and paint them. I found that easy to do and a long series of pictures emerged, which went on for about seven years and periodically after that. I found that I could orientate myself in emotional crises by painting, to which I added imaginary conversations with some of the figures which emerged. At first it seemed that my quite serious mental disorganization was due to the painting, but I soon got it right. Baynes seemed to think the way to deal with the mass of material was to introduce a considerable amount of education, and he suggested books I should read. They did not benefit me and I think they were more his interest than mine, although I found Jung's seminars on vision absorbing and often relevant. Then it came about that as I could not pay much for my analysis Baynes got a conscience and suggested that he would take my material as payment, since he wanted to use it in a book he was writing. I agreed, although with considerable hesitation. It was not a satisfactory solution: one disadvantage was that I felt obliged to keep on producing pictures to keep up payments! Sometimes Baynes invited me down to his house at Byfleet in Surrey and there he read me chapters out of his book. I listened, thought it very ingenious and that increased my idealization of him. It did not, however, seem to have much relevance to my conflicts, though I was flattered by the astonishing things I was told my unconscious produced: analogies were drawn between my productions, Kundalini yoga, alchemy and the like. Only the subject of the two women seemed to me especially relevant, but here again his method was educative rather than analytic. He gave me an account of Jung's comparable experience in some detail. I do not think that did much more than increase my sense of inflation in doing what Jung had done, but I succeeded in keeping enough in touch with reality. My relation to Molly deteriorated, however, and I think that was contributed to by the absence of transference analysis.

My work with Baynes did not end satisfactorily and after about another year and six months, with a break in the middle of it, I gave up; my doing so was supported by Jung in a very characteristic way. When he was over in England lecturing I went to see him by appointment and was shown up to his bedroom, where he was dressing for dinner. The informality did not seem to matter in the least, and indeed put me at my ease as I told him what I had come about and how difficult it had become with Baynes. There was no beating about the bush: I thought I heard him mumble 'Yes I bet it is,' and then he said clearly, 'I saw at once that he was identified with your material and if you want to do so you had better get out'. He then raised the question of whom I should see. I wanted to start with Hilde Kirsch but he did not accept this at once – could I not think of anybody else? However, I had objections to each of the ones he mentioned, so to Hilde Kirsch I went, after some hesitation on her part – it was a great relief. I later understood the hesitations, for I was the first patient she had ever treated!

My work with Baynes had become further complicated because it gave rise to gossip. Baynes himself had shown my material to Jung and he told me so; he also said that Jung had objected strongly to what he was doing. He asked me what I thought and I said he should not drop the project as Jung wanted him to do; it was part of our agreement anyway and I thought he should fight off Jung's views. Baynes thought that 'peculiar', if I remember the word he used. This state of affairs got around and I received condolences, especially at being a published case, which it was said would be used against me. My good friend Joseph Wheelwright was especially vigorous in his views and thought I had received a rotten deal from my analysts (he included Hilde Kirsch in that – wrongly, as I thought).

Before assessing my work with Hilde Kirsch I must correct the impression that work with Baynes was unproductive. I have mentioned the 'breakthrough' which took place almost at once. That released my imagination and I painted pictures almost every day. In addition I studied dreams and held conversations with imaginary figures. Most of this activity went on in my spare time on my own. In the interviews with Baynes he acted as a supervisor of my progress, making suggestions and drawing parallels with myths and the experience of others, especially Jung. This period gave me a firm conviction as to the reality of unconscious processes and the relative autonomy of its products. During this period I experienced synchronicities and once I believed that I encountered a poltergeist, but these events were of a rather trivial kind. I must add that my discoveries had an inspirational effect although I cannot quite define how that came about with any precision. Another benefit was that I knew about my 'inner world' as distinct from outer reality.

When I started with Hilde Kirsch I had developed a method of proceeding. I went along with my dream book, my painting and records of 'internal conversations'. With Baynes we had sat in chairs opposite each other; Hilde thought sitting at a table better. In contrast to Baynes she was a good listener and did not interfere with my flow of talk. When she did talk it was quite different from my previous experience. Some of it was analytic in nature but there was something more important: she had a good capacity for containment and so I felt safe, and her statements seemed to come right out of her experience – they represented genuine emotional experience that she had assimilated. So, under her competent care, I began to organize my inner world better and it lost its compulsive character. Correspondingly my outer life became more stable. One day, however, I took along a sexual dream about her and everything began to change. First she said I should go along to have an interview with her husband, James Kirsch, also a Jungian analyst, which I did – it was unproductive. Then she invited me to have dinner with her husband present, which I found embarrassing; besides I only remember the excellent fillet steak which she cooked. I half-realized she was evading my transference and acting on her countertransference. Like Baynes she paid little or no attention to my transference, and indeed once said she did not think I had one and what did I think? I did not reply.

The work continued. Then she did something else: she suggested that I hold a seminar on child therapy at her house for a number of analytical psychologists, who formed a group round herself and her husband. I appreciated that she was supporting my interest in child therapy, but it meant that working on my transference was impossible. I reduced my interviews with her to once a week and soon stopped regular ones altogether. I was glad that my relation with her continued until she moved with her family to the USA soon after the 'phoney war' began. She explained to me that it would be safer there, especially for her small son. This seemed to me reasonable but in my unconscious I felt abandoned, which I did not mention to her.

There were some consequences of my work with Baynes and Hilde Kirsch which were to prove important in directing my researches afterwards: neither analyst seemed to know how to analyse my childhood, nor did they understand about transference. I made both these fields of study my particular concern. Another effect was that I never used amplification as Baynes had done with me, and indeed largely eliminated it from my practice. Finally there was the influence of being published as a case: nearly all the material I was to publish later was collected from children – they could not be identified as I could be in Baynes's book, *Mythology of the Soul*, which was published in 1940. I think that I did not publish much material from my adult cases because of this, although I think this was mistaken.

Before starting my work with Hilde Kirsch, Molly and I had returned from Barking and had rented a house in St John's Wood. Our fortunes had taken a turn for the better: I had a post at the Child Guidance Clinic as head of a unit and Molly had joined the staff of *Vogue*. So it might have been thought that all was set fair for our futures. Materially that was so, but our marriage was deteriorating. I do not think that Molly ever became promiscuous but she had lovers, while I was not above reproach by any means. None the less, because of the rather free views about sexual behaviour held amongst us at that time, our behaviour was no more than a symptom of degeneration in our marriage relationship. Our marriage did not develop as it might have done at this time, despite our best intentions. Today it is quite usual for couples to marry when they are still students or for the wife to be the wage earner. This was the state of affairs in our marriage at first, and at this period we would both have needed to develop and deepen the meaning of the marriage for it to survive. Molly wanted to and went into analysis, but it was not enough, while my analysis had not helped me in that part of my development. As a result of our situation my identity as a male became disturbed and the attempt to correct it led to quarrels. I do not want to give the impression that my first marriage was not valuable; indeed, there was much in it that was rich and productive, Max being its culmination. It also led to each of us establishing ourselves professionally but in divergent directions; she in journalism and me in analytical psychology.

In St John's Wood my relationship with Jungians developed and Baynes, mistakenly, pitchforked me into becoming chairman of the Analytical Psychology Club. I did not feel at home in that position, since I felt myself to be only a very junior member. He did so, however, for better or worse, and Molly and I agreed to hold Club meetings in our house. Amongst the members were two Americans, Joseph Wheelwright and Joseph Henderson. They were training to be doctors on Jung's insistence, and had both decided to do that in England, choosing to become students at St Bartholomew's Hospital. Each lived in a flat by the river in Chelsea. Our relationship became close and has lasted over the years. They were strikingly unlike each other and yet they were to form a powerful team in San Francisco, together building up the Jungian Institute there. Wheelwright announced himself as an extroverted, feeling type and he took me by storm, as it were; Henderson was an introvert and it was I, rather than he, who valued our relationship. I learned much about Jung's psychology of types from these two and also how valuable and enjoyable good friendships could be.

Concurrently my relationship with a woman called Frieda Hoyle was deepening. We had first met at the clinic, where she was training to be a psychiatric social worker. I admired her work with mothers, which was subtle and deep, and almost in a different class

Frieda

from other workers. I used to hold evening sessions for adolescents and would eat my supper in the garden. One evening she came over and talked to me – I fell in love with her then; it was the sort of love that was the heir to what I had felt for my mother and then for Ruth Childers. This meant that I wanted marriage in a deep sense. Out of guilt we tried to separate and when she had trained Frieda took a post in Leicester, but it did not work out. Molly knew about it and would have continued with our marriage, allowing my relation with Frieda to carry on. I could not do that. As a relationship with loving affection in it, our marriage had been fruitful. There had been quarrelling but not of a malignant kind, and it had produced a fine boy in whom we both delighted, but it was more of a companionship and not the marriage I was urgently looking for, which it would be possible to achieve with Frieda.

During this period, from 1935 until the war, Jung came over to England three times, once to give the Tavistock Lectures in 1935, once to speak at the Abernethian Society at Bart's in 1936 and a third time as President of the International General Medical Society for Psychotherapy when it held a conference at Oxford in 1938 or 1939. Each of these occasions was memorable. When he came over to Bart's, the Analytical Psychology Club wanted him to spend some time with them. Jung agreed, as long as the meeting was small. That was not at all Baynes's idea, for he wanted to make a big occasion of it. The Club Committee contested him but he was too powerful, and a large hall was rented, the occasion suitably advertised and Jung spoke to a crammed auditorium. It was the first time I saw Jung at his worst. Baynes delivered a flowery introduction which made me feel sick and then Jung read his paper in a dull monotonous voice. There was no discussion worth mentioning. I sat in the gallery near Mrs Jung, whom I had not seen before (it was after the Second World War that I got to know her better and she showed interest in my studies of childhood). The Tavistock Lectures, which were more like a number of seminars, were a glorious contrast. Jung was at his best, speaking to a mostly eclectic audience.

I trained, in as much as I ever had any training, at the Tavistock Clinic (I think then called The Institute of Medical Psychology), and my application to the Institute for membership was deferred. The authorities were bound to do this because I had been accused of

Photo: William McGuire

Mrs Jung and Dr Jung

immoral practices. I had suggested to a patient that I was treating that he might pick up a prostitute. It was a repetition of Baynes's proposal to me and not at all appropriate. Nevertheless, I did not like the eclectic and rather moralistic atmosphere of the Institute, which played down the transference and which was promoting brief psychotherapy. So when I was told that if I waited a short time and then applied, I was likely to be accepted, I did not take up the matter, preferring to remain outside the Institute's jurisdiction.

I mention this because I think that some of the contents of Jung's seminars were influenced by what he knew of his audience. Some of his remarks on the transference, for instance, much objected to by my Jungian colleagues, were just what the members of the Institute would have liked to hear (I do not think that any psychoanalysts were present, although Dr Wilfred Bion was – he would not then have been a psychoanalyst). Jung recognized the inevitability of transferences but he did not like an intense one, and asserted that a transference was not necessary for therapy to take place. Nevertheless, the whole occasion was alive and the discussion vigorous. Jung's exposition, which covered his experimental researches, the theory of the complex, psychological types and the archetypes, was brilliant and clear. At times Jung was downright controversial and sometimes rude. Much of the seminars' vitality is lost in the printed version, which has been heavily edited. He was especially firm against those who wanted to make out that he only discovered speculative theory. On the contrary, he asserted, he was not interested in theory but in facts. The Jungians in the audience gave him little support and Antonia Wolff, a close colleague of Jung's who had come with him from Zurich, was very indignant about it. I wished I had thought myself sufficiently senior to do as she wished and support him, but I did not and felt ashamed.

In the fourth seminar Jung started on the amplification of an archetypal dream. It became elaborate and I think bewildered many members of the audience. He would have continued that in the fifth and last meeting, but the chairman intervened and asked him to speak about the transference, which he did. This last meeting was an important occasion and, I think, disposed of the idea that Jung could be allowed to fade out as a dissident psychoanalyst.

On Jung's third visit to England he came as President of the International General Medical Society for Psychotherapy, which was holding a conference in Oxford. The occasion was complicated because he was being suspected of anti-Semitism and Nazi sympathies, so he had to defend himself. I met him only briefly and quite casually and we talked. I do not remember the content of our conversation but I do remember the sense of intimacy again, yet this time as if I was his son. Jung himself did not read a paper to the conference, but he agreed to answer written questions submitted to him from the floor. The idea was that he would present himself well in this way and so ward off some of his detractors. I do not think it was a success. The real Jung did not appear: he was guarded, dull and uninspired.

During the conference he was given a doctorate by the university; I believe he was the first psychologist, and certainly the first psychotherapist, ever to receive that honour. Jung took such an important occasion with a grain of salt. His reply to the Chancellor was flowery and in bad taste by English standards, but that could easily be forgiven since he was a foreigner. However, as he came down off the platform on which the ceremony had taken place and walked down an aisle between the assembled multitude he gave what seemed to be a gigantic wink at C.A. Meier, who was standing beside me, so that we were both convulsed with laughter. It appealed to both of us because of our disrespect for the Establishment, to which, of course, we both belonged. It reminded me of my Uncle George who, when he was chairman of the Cambridge County Council early in the present century, hung the Red Flag above the Union Jack on Labour Day. Rebels will remain so and seek ways of expressing their natures one way or another.

11 TRANSITION: NOTTINGHAM, WARTIME

In the late thirties a child guidance clinic was starting up in Nottingham and appointments for a child guidance team were advertised. There was a part-time post for a consultant, which I was fortunate enough to get and Frieda was appointed as the psychiatric social worker. It meant commuting between London and Nottingham, but Frieda took a small house and so we could be together for part of each week. It turned out that Dr Newth, the medical officer of health, was a pleasure to work with, especially when he took over, with Frieda's assistance, the sorting out of cases for treatment or educational management. Newth and I held weekly lunch-time meetings to discuss our work. In addition Lawrey Hawkey, the psychologist, was interested in analytic methods and I trained her to become a psychotherapist, and a very good one at that. I had hoped that she would continue her liaison with the schools but, as I had witnessed before, she found psychotherapy so much more to her liking that she asked to be relieved of her other commitments to become a full-time psychotherapist. So, as Frieda had also been analysed, the clinic became a real psychotherapeutic unit whose members were united in their aims. Only the new psychologist, appointed in the place of Lawrey Hawkey, was different. He worked only in the schools and did not integrate with the rest of the team, seeming uninterested and difficult to contact. It was only many years later I learned that my view of him was wrong and that our work had largely contributed to his entering Jungian psychotherapy for himself.

Another project presented itself at this time. The Common-wealth Foundation was negotiating with St Bartholomew's Hospital to start a child guidance unit in the paediatric department, and William Moodie, Director of the London Child Guidance Clinic, put me up as a suitable child psychiatrist. I was given every reason to suppose that I would be appointed. I knew Harris, the consultant paediatrician at Bart's, and he, though ambivalent in principle, was likely to accept the addition to his department. It would have been a very prestigious appointment but the outbreak of war put an end to that. As might have been expected, the war also disrupted my work in London. The clinic closed down, under protest by some of us, and eventually its rump moved to Cambridge. Those of us who wanted to continue in London opened another clinic inspired by Dr Posthuma – I joined it and so did Mrs Jean Rhees, who subsequently trained and became an analyst. It did not last long, for lack of funds.

I do not know why I was not enlisted by the army. I was told to join a team of psychiatrists and attended two meetings, but heard no more. I suppose that a child psychiatrist was better employed looking after children, as indeed proved to be the case. Consequently, during the 'phoney war' period I had time on my hands which was filled up by William Moodie's generosity: he handed over a few of his patients and an appointment as consultant to the Sunshine Homes for partially sighted and blind children. I learned something from visiting the homes but was much more upset by the state of the children and the way they were treated. Furthermore, I did not feel that I was being much use. The National Institute for the Blind announced that they were planning more such homes, and when I protested that they should first train the staff to man them, I was told that my services would no longer be required. I very much appreciated Moodie's tolerance of my behaviour when he returned after the war.

In the rest of my free time I drafted a version of my first book, containing what I had learned about children up to that time. I took *The Life of Childhood* up to Nottingham, where Frieda and I worked hard on it. I knew that my writing of English was poor and the contents disorderly in many respects. We fought over it, since Frieda was a discerning critic and what she said was often far from complimentary! She could write English naturally, or so it seemed, and I learned how to do it well enough, for my purposes, from her. It took some time before I dared to submit it for publication to Routledge and Kegan Paul and I was surprised and delighted when it was accepted – it was published in 1944, and sold better than any of my other books.

During this wartime period I wrote to Eric Strauss, who was the consultant psychiatrist at Bart's, and whom I knew, saying that I would like to work in his department provided I did not have to see more than ten patients in an afternoon session. I thought he agreed so I started to work with him, but my limit was soon broken and it seemed a rather fruitless occupation. Indeed, I thought most of any psychotherapy that took place was conducted in the waiting-room where patients gossiped freely with each other. In addition, when a transference developed, it was impossible to manage it satisfactorily using the methods I had developed, so when the work in Nottingham increased I retired. However, Strauss must have thought that what I did was not so unsatisfactory, for after the war he invited me to become a consultant at Bart's, but I was too much involved with building up the Jungian centre (the Society of Analytical Psychology), which had started by then and of which I was an active member. This was a step in decision-making that was new to me. I had previously taken a largely passive part in my career, taking up opportunities as they were presented to me; it was the failures that impressed me. Now I decided what I meant to do, even if that meant turning down an opportunity to establish myself as a respected member of the Establishment. At the time analytical psychology was a relative backwater and its position still had to be established.

The work in Nottingham continued, with the addition of appointments to the Sheffield and Chesterfield Child Guidance Clinics. In Sheffield the clinic had run into difficulties and had become a centre of scandal. It had all come about because local authorities had been compelled by act of Parliament to open up clinics without training staff to do the work. In a way the Yorkshire folk were right, for some of the efforts at treatment were decidedly odd to say the least. However, I had sympathy for the staff who, in their efforts to help, had read up bits of Freud and Melanie Klein and dealt out sexual interpretations in such a way that the children went home and told their parents, in a garbled way, what the therapist had said. It was this which had given rise to the scandal. I took to the Yorkshire people almost at once: they were outspoken, not to say insulting, but it was all so warm that it was not difficult to convince them that their fears of immoral practices by the clinic staff were unfounded, and the scandal departed.

The clinic at Chesterfield was no problem. The psychiatrist, whose name I never knew, had retired and I replaced him (or was it her?). The staff was competent and one of Margaret Lowenfeld's therapists was doing good work. I was interested because I had previously been in quite close contact with Dr Lowenfeld, who had started a clinic and a training for child psychotherapists in the method she had devised. I had been the external examiner for that training for a short period, and had briefly adopted part of her methods. However, serious doubts grew up in my mind about her therapeutic techniques. She developed her now famous sand tray method, which provided a large number of toys and invited children to use them in the sand tray as they felt inclined. This, used in connection with her mosaic test, was a good way of diagnosing some of the children's conflicts. Lowenfeld had found in the sand tray 'pictures' a number of arrangements which referred to archetypal configurations and this was one reason for our mutual interest: would it be desirable to collect toys having mythological characteristics? But it was not on these grounds, though I thought them a bit superficial, that I had serious doubts. My doubts centred on her antipathy to the transference, which was not merely played down but as far as possible was prevented from being manifested in relation to her therapists. However, I had not had experience of how Lowenfeld's trainees used or adapted her methods. One of them, Miss Trail, was a good therapist and could develop a good relation with her cases – it was that, I thought, which produced her results more than the rather elaborate apparatus. I discussed this with her but she was not to be weaned from the toys and sand tray. I had a similar experience with other therapists who used it – they all seemed to get stuck with it. To some extent I had found a much modified version of the technique useful, but I eventually discarded it as I found transference analysis more fruitful.

I now come to a most important experience with children in this wartime period. In 1942 I was appointed to a consultant post with the task of helping with those evacuee children who had not been able to settle in billets. Hostels had already been set up to accommodate them and I only needed to supervise them with the help of a psychiatric social worker, Mrs Hicking. She worked with great skill and effectiveness so that once she had located a trouble spot – which usually consisted in the child and the matron being incompatible – all I had to do was to confirm that a child needed to be moved to another hostel where he or she was more likely to fit in.

In addition, a special 'therapeutic hostel' for the most difficult children had been set up in Burton Joyce, a village in Nottingham-shire. The task in such a hostel was different, in that I was supposed to conduct psychotherapy there. Unwisely, as it turned out, I agreed to do that. I asked for a special room to be constructed and gave specifications about how it should be decorated so that paintings on the wall could be wiped off. That was delayed for some reason and, again unwisely, I started off with one or two children before the room was completed – even before it had a lock on the door. I must have tried to investigate some rather obvious sexual fantasies that one of them produced and then left for that day. The next week I was confronted on a piece of open ground by a gang of boys who pelted me with coke: I defended myself with a wide stick. The battle ended with the children and me in quite good heart, thought I had some blood on my face to mop up. I did not understand what this was all about, especially when I was asked, to my annoyance, not to go to the hostel for a temporary period while members of the Board of Control investigated; they soon found quite extensive bruises on children inflicted by the superintendent, who was consequently discharged. He was replaced by a Miss Maw and I was allowed to go back with instructions not to attempt psychotherapy! Much later I asked the doctor in charge why that was. It appeared that the walls of the room had been found covered with sexual pictures – the boys must have got into the room when I was not there and drawn them. The doctor was quite astonished and remarked that if he had known earlier that it was nothing to do with me the scandal need not have occurred.

The atmosphere of the hostel was transformed by Miss Maw and I arranged that I should come once a week to discuss any matters that she wanted to bring up. Each week I came at tea-time and joined the children in their meal. I also wandered round the hostel talking to the boys and observing what was going on: it all seemed very satisfactory, especially in that the boys were far more happy and friendly than under the previous superintendent. It was probably because of the way I behaved that I soon established good relations with Miss Maw and she began to talk freely. One problem was the hostile attitude of the local inhabitants. That soon changed when they were invited to see what was going on and found what a happy community now existed. Also there was less delinquency outside the hostel, since we did all we could to keep bad behaviour within the hostel grounds in order not to offend the villagers: that also enlisted their good will.

But the policy of keeping the children in the hostel presented difficulties; for example, some of the boys took a dislike to the local schoolmaster and eventually would not go to school at all – they remained in the hostel. That incensed the teacher, who came round to give Miss Maw instruction in how to manage such children – he was outraged at finding them in the hostel. Eventually he decided to come round and fetch them himself. The boys saw him coming and, presumably guessing his intention, went up on to the roof, put their feet on the gutter and challenged him to come and fetch them, leaving him looking foolish on the ground. After that he recognized that the boys were unusually difficult, and he became our ally and even our friend, for he began talking about himself. It appeared that he himself had been a delinquent boy and had been sent to an approved school. After that he had made good and the school in Burton Joyce, where he had done a good job raising the standards to everybody's satisfaction, was his pride and justification. Our boys were a blot on his competence. With his change of attitude the boys went back to school – I should probably add 'for most of the time' for I cannot believe they did not truant sometimes.

The children were 'difficult' but they were never dull and sometimes what they did was a joy to watch. Once Miss Maw became ill and took to her bed. Everybody immediately became well behaved, as quiet as mice and helpful too: they visited the bedroom to enquire whether she wanted their company, which she did, and they performed small services like carrying her food upstairs, and so on. In all this they were sensitive and never intrusive. I learned an enormous amount about children, and about their psychopathology, for the hostel contained all sorts of abnormalities. I also learned what a psychotherapeutic atmosphere could do for them, even the psychotic ones. I discovered that there was a difference between a real delinquent, who may have come from a criminal background where crime and prison were part of the rhythm of life, and a neurotic one. And much more besides.

I had another experience whilst supervising hostels which astounded me at the time, although my psychiatric social worker had come across such incidents before. One day she and I were summoned to a hostel where we found the doors off their hinges, the windows broken and, a curious detail, the marks of dirty hands all over the walls and ceiling of the main room. The hostel was filthy and there were no boys at all to be seen; they had all deserted and the matron was sitting there in amazement at what the boys had done. She was a perfectly good matron under ordinary circumstances, but something had enraged the children and bedlam broke out. We never found out what had happened nor did we enquire much, for dealing with the immediate situation was imperative. We detected the leader and introduced him to Miss Maw, who decided she could take him. The matron of the destroyed hostel was moved elsewhere and functioned well as far as I know, and the scene of the disaster was eventually reconstituted with new staff. There was no further call for assistance.

The 'leader' lasted long enough in our therapeutic hostel for us to observe some obsessional tendencies which kept him relatively stable. He then became manic and attacked Miss Maw, who fought him back and as he was a big boy, I thought he might cause serious harm. Should we move him? Miss Maw did not want to give up, however. After the attack the boy became depressed and I did not like the look of it, especially as there were potentially suicidal tendencies, so he was moved to another hostel that was run on 'public school' lines. There a man who had strict rules was in

control: prefects, badges for achievement, football teams, the lot –
including a cane used sparingly. I thought that the firm environment
would support the obsessional parts of the boy's character. The
move was a success – the boy became a pillar of the hostel society
and later in life a sergeant major in the army!

These are some of the experiences which taught me much more
about the shadow side of life, both personal and social. It had been
fascinating, emotional, and sometimes dangerous. Frieda's unquali-
fied and warm support during the hostel crisis bound us even closer
together, and music also contributed: I kept playing Sibelius's First
Symphony and Tchaikovsky's First Piano Concerto – they chan-
nelled my emotions in an almost miraculous fashion.

Returning to my thinking about children during this tumultuous
time, I was developing the idea that, in violation of Jungian theory,
self theory was important in infancy and childhood, when Frieda
showed me pictures made by a child she had been treating. The
little girl had been returned from evacuation to her parents because
of her sexual behaviour. She was somewhat disintegrated by events
during evacuation, the details of which were never disclosed,
presumably because they were too 'shocking' to mention. The little
girl evidently got much benefit from her relation with Frieda and
painted a sequence of mandalas, classical symbols of the self in
Jungian circles. They were published in *The Life of Childhood*. They
were evidence for my thesis that the self, in Jung's sense, was an
active factor in child development, whereas Jungians thought it
only became important in the second half of life. The self was not
a feature of childhood and consequently the study of childhood was
of no importance and any psychopathology was entirely due to the
parents, especially the mother. My growing experience was
showing that thesis to be false. I was demolishing the idea that
neurotic and psychotic children could only be treated indirectly,
that is, through treatment of parents. The case of the evacuated
children became confirmation of my ideas: there were virtually no
parents available anyway, so that parental influence in the present
situation had ceased altogether and the question of treating them
was meaningless. Yet the children showed an astonishing capacity
to recover from whatever had happened before. The conclusion
that children had a self that was separate from their parents was

growing, with evidence to back it up – the thesis was taking hold of me at this time. It was to form the basis of a Jungian theory of child development and child analysis.

It was during this period that Frieda and I married, and that consolidated our relationship. For me it ended the mourning for my mother. Frieda made a home, as she had done for her two boys, Tony and Pat, from her previous marriage. Our marriage became the foundation for all my subsequent achievements – a large statement, but I believe it to be true. I took up what was to be the difficult task of being a step-father to Tony and Pat. I had conceived that talented people went to university and it puzzled me a great deal that neither of them considered it a possibility. At the time this was incredible to me, nor did either of them seem to want to have a career – in the end both went into business. They were difficult for me to make contact with, probably because their own father showed no serious interest in them. Also, the Hoyle family was dominated by a rich grandmother, who paid their school fees and provided a rather inadequate sum for them to live on, until Frieda eventually became a psychiatric social worker and began to gain more financial independence. Thus the boys lived in the atmosphere of a matriarchy and did not know what to do with a father, except as an annexe to their mother and powerful grandmother. During the period we are considering they were both at boarding school or conscripted. Tony, the elder, went into the army and Pat into the Navy, so it was mostly on holidays, which Frieda made most enjoyable, that I came across them.

During this period Max was first evacuated to Essex and then, partly because neither Molly nor I was able to give him a sufficiently stable background and partly because of wartime dangers, we decided to send him out to Jamaica where Molly's brother and his wife were living. So Molly and Max departed and arrived safely. Unfortunately, finding that Max was well looked after and settled in Jamaica, Molly decided to return to England to remarry. Her boat was sunk, tragically, and I heard no more of her – she was presumed to have been drowned.

I missed Max but I think Jamaica was a good solution, for his uncle's marriage had proved childless and Max was made very welcome. He was, indeed, treated royally, as we found out when he got back. There was a black nurse who had looked after him; she picked up his clothes when he threw them on the floor and even put toothpaste on his tooth-brush. When he came back to live with Frieda and me in London after the war was over, Max expected Frieda to do the same as the nurse! He made a good relation with his uncle, who was a forester, and went with him on his expeditions into the forests, which included mountain climbing. Back in London after the war Max talked on and on to us about these mountains, the like of which England could never match. Eventually we took him by car to Switzerland over the Gotthard pass to Lake Maggiore and back again over the mountains to Annecy. After that he recognized that Europe, at least, had mountains worthy of consideration!

The other feature of Max's time in Jamaica was his school reports, on one of which was the statement: 'Max does not know the meaning of the term obey'. When I asked him about this he told me: 'Well, the mathematics master did not explain himself very well and if I asked questions he became annoyed so there was nothing to do but bore holes in the wall'. That contributed to our sending him to Dartington Hall school in Devon, where the masters and mistresses were all intelligent and little emphasis was laid on discipline. The only complaint from Max was that you had to do such awful things before anybody would take any notice! He enjoyed his school life, however, and went on to Trinity College, Cambridge, to my great satisfaction. He has been – and is – a fine son to have fathered, though much of his early life was lived away from me and I was dependent on infrequent meetings and correspondence, filled in with what he told us later.

12 LONDON AND ANALYTICAL PSYCHOLOGY

In 1943 Erna Rosenbaum, a Jungian analyst and a founder member of the Society of Analytical Psychologists, telephoned me in Nottingham asking me to come down to London to help organize a group of analysts who wanted to form a professional institute. As the bombing of London had apparently ceased, Frieda and I decided to come and explore the possibilities. There were two considerations. First I had to discover more about the situation: earlier efforts to get analysts to collaborate had not been easy. I had participated in the earlier discussions but had not continued in them when I went to Nottingham, so I did not know what had happened in the meantime. During the earlier efforts Godwin Baynes had been the leader but now he was dead. I assumed that an Englishman with sufficient status to act as a persona was required, especially by the analysts who had migrated from Germany and did not have English medical degrees. The second consideration was whether it was desirable to leave the relative safety of Nottingham. On both counts it appeared worthwhile to make the change: here was a group of senior analysts who were unanimous in wanting to start a training in analytical psychology and they evidently thought I was the person to organize it. In addition, before his death Baynes had persuaded a Mrs Marged Welch, who had been to Zurich and after an analysis there had returned to England to continue her work with Baynes, to put down one thousand pounds to finance the project. So I met her and her husband, gaining their support.

Frieda looked for a house and found one in St Katherine's Precinct, Regent's Park. The building had been bombed and was in a parlous condition but the landlords (the Crown Commissioners) agreed to put it in liveable order. That done, we moved in with what furniture we had in our possession. It was all clean and tidy. Frieda remarked: 'I have a feeling that it will never be so clean again'. That night a flying bomb fell on St Katherine's Hospital over the road in the park. For some reason we had decided to sleep in the hall and I woke up to see the front door almost waltzing down the passage; it leant gracefully up against the wall when its dance had ended. I went out to see whether I could be of any help at the hospital, but rescue operations were well under way with a team working under powerful arc lamps. So I returned to survey the damage to our house: it was not as bad as might have been expected. Most of the windows had been blown out, but no ceilings had come down, though there was much dust. Repairs could be made quite quickly and that was done the following day. It was not long before the windows were blown out again and again and again, and the men who came to repair them started to joke about the frequency with which we had to call on their aid. It appeared that Regent's Park was a 'parking place' for the missiles as, indeed, a friend at the ministry told us was the case. Flying bombs were far more unnerving than rockets: you could hear the brute coming along, it would cut out and then there was an anxious interval before the explosion took place. It became so hard to tolerate that Frieda departed and I was at the Precinct only during the day. None the less I succeeded in building up a small practice and went up to Nottingham each week till the end of the war, by which time the Jungian Society was well under way.

Efforts to start the Centre for Analytical Psychology – as it was then called – went forward slowly. First of all it was necessary to decide whether the Analytical Psychology Club should be part of it, and there was a good deal of disagreeableness in the discussion. Prominent amongst the Club's objections was the suspicion of domination by the analysts. The Club wished to dissociate their members from the 'taint' of professionalism, though quite a number of them practised psychotherapy. It was true that the analysts wanted to exercise some control over the Club members, who were in fact performing quasi-professional activities. In order to try and reach a decision I eventually wrote a paper setting out the reasons why the new body was needed but separating the Club from the professional activities, thus proposing a single unit with two departments. In spite of my efforts not enough of the Club members were persuaded to join in, and so the analysts went ahead on their own to form the Society of Analytical Psychology. Having settled that matter we decided to draw up Articles and Memoranda of Association so that we could become a charity, and benefit financially. I found the work on this fascinating and the sponsors, Mr and Mrs Welch, and their solicitor expressed astonishment that I took so much trouble – I did so because I wanted to understand the structure and functioning of the Society and the legal requirements of a charity.

The founder members were Gerhard Adler, Culver Barker, Erna Rosenbaum, myself and Frieda Fordham (though she was not an analyst at the time), Phillip Metman, Lotte Paulsen and Robert Moody. Marged Welch lent us part of her house in St John's Wood where we could hold meetings and start a clinic. It was a small group and I learned a lot about how difficult it was for analysts to get along with each other – Adler and Rosenbaum in particular did not seem to see eye to eye on much. At the start, however, they sank their differences, and discussions on clinical material were quite vivid, especially when it came to training. We decided that we wanted to provide cases for the students to analyse under the supervision of a senior analyst. The question of supervision became a central issue and Jung was consulted. He gave, somewhat to my surprise, his qualified approval to our proposals to separate supervision and analysis. My impression had been that he did not like professional societies of analysts at all, nor systematic clinical training. He wanted to base analysis on vocation: a prospective analyst would discover his talent during his analysis, which was therefore the nub of any training given. An additional requirement was a considerable knowledge of myths and religious practices, which Jung himself provided in his erudite and inspiring seminars delivered in Zurich. Jung also seemed to be in favour of medical training. It was partly because of his supposed views and the fact that we intended to sponsor lay analysts, that we made it necessary for the chairman of our society to be a doctor, a requirement only recently waived.

My reason for thinking that Jung favoured a medical qualification was his recommendation that the two prospective analysts, Joseph Wheelwright and Joseph Henderson, should qualify in medicine – they had come over from the USA to do so. At the same time Jung recognized many lay analysts, amongst whom were Antonia Wolff, Mrs Jung and many others. I do not know why he appeared so inconsistent but he may have thought that in the States a medical qualification would be an advantage, as it then was in England, so the two Americans may have been a special case.

A further special requirement for analysts had been that they go out to Zurich to study there, either with Jung himself or one of his assistants. In London we decided we would not make going to Zurich necessary for qualification, since we wanted to take full responsibility for what we did. We also decided that we would accept, besides medical trainees, psychologists and psychiatric social workers. This decision has been amply justified by the results: good analysts have developed out of these disciplines. I would like to add in parenthesis that one of our best analysts had no pre-training qualifications at all. Our project was a pioneering one. We were the first group of Jungian analysts in the world to form a society having the aim of promoting analytical psychology and training analysts. Our emphasis on the practice of analysis, by asking candidates to analyse two patients under supervision, was a new departure for Jungians. Our enterprise and much of its procedure has been widely followed.

In all this I found myself becoming something of a leader. I say 'found myself' because I had defects as a Jungian. I was something of a vocational analyst, although, as I have mentioned, I did take the training at the Institute of Medical Psychology (now the Tavistock Clinic). I had not studied in Zurich nor did I intend to: my life in London was becoming far too rich and I was sufficiently accepted by the Jungians and others in England. It was partly because of this, but also because I held that we were serving a science, that I insisted on calling our society the Society of Analytical Psychology and not the C. G. Jung Institute. As it turned out that was a wise decision because of the personality cult that threatened to develop at one time. My 'defect' was partly felt by myself but was also used by the 'authentic' Jungians (Gerhard Adler, Culver Barker and Erna Rosenbaum), who wanted to have more influence than they in fact had: they felt that I did not have the true Jungian spirit. In spite of all this my position as leader seemed just to come about and I enjoyed the power of it and, to a lesser extent, the administrative work.

My identification with the Society led to two decisions. Soon after the end of the war William Moodie approached me to ask whether I would be interested in taking over the London Child Guidance Clinic and at the same time apply for the post of consultant psychiatrist at University College Hospital. I said I was uncertain about the Clinic but would be interested in UCH and I went for interviews. At one of these a portly doctor said he hoped that I was not 'too Jungian'. That annoyed me, but more importantly, as the interview went on, it transpired that the appointment would have involved my being chief consultant to the adult department as well as its child guidance clinic. As I did not think I had sufficient experience in adult psychiatry I withdrew. I am deeply grateful for Dr Moodie's confidence in me, which I met with on other occasions. I wondered, however, whether he grasped how critical I was of the child guidance team method; I do not think he was all that happy with it himself and he may have thought it needed a shake-up. To have accepted either of these posts would have involved me in work which I could have done but which would have gone against the grain.

Another offer – not quite so explicit – came from Eric Strauss, the psychiatric consultant at Bart's where I had worked for a short time during the war. He told me he wanted a Jungian consultant on his staff. I told him that I was too committed to the SAP and in building up analytical psychology in Britain to accept his proposition. Once again I could have been 'made', but as a psychiatrist and not an analyst. These events made me reflect on my ambition. It did not seem that I had much of it in a professional sense. I was rather seeking to find out what suited me and what did not. These two occasions were new: previously I had not had a choice, this time I had. Either I worked in a teaching hospital where analysis was all but impossible, or else I went out into the wilderness where I could work as I wanted.

There were other important developments. Herbert Read, who knew my father, approached me with an offer of the editorship of the *Collected Works* of Jung. He did not tell me at the time but I discovered, many years later, that the idea had come from no less a person than Jung himself! The idea of becoming an editor astounded me and I expostulated that I knew nothing about editing. Read said that I could easily learn what was necessary and when I pointed out that I knew no German he retorted that R.F.C. Hull, the translator, would look after that. So after considerable hesitation and after consulting James Strachey, editor of Freud's *Standard Edition*, who did not seem to think I was unsuitable, and after meeting Hull, whom I liked and with whom I thought I could work, I accepted.

Of course I knew there would be objections from more orthodox Jungians but they did not surface at once. Nevertheless, there was one aspirant for the part of translator. That became apparent when a translation by Barbara Hanna was sent to me, together with a translation of the same piece by Hull. I was asked to make a judgement as to which was the better. There was no comparison: Hull's translation was infinitely better. The decision must have been deeply disappointing to Barbara but there was never a trace of resentment on her part.

Read's proposition was based on financial support from the Bollingen Foundation in New York so I soon met Jack Barret, their President, and also Paul Mellon, who evidently wanted to see what I was like. The Bollingen Foundation had been established in 1945 by Paul Mellon and his first wife Mary. His benefaction enabled the *Collected Works* to be published and numerous research scholarships to be financed. Many other publications, relating to religion, symbolism, anthropology, myth and poetry, were supported. Later preliminary meetings took place in Zurich between Jung, Jack Barret, Herbert Read and myself.

Gradually, criticisms of the project came to the surface and they culminated during one Eranos conference held at Ascona in Switzerland: they focused on doubts about my suitability as editor and, though these corresponded to my own doubts, I felt hurt by having them treated as though they disqualified me. In the end, as a compromise, an editorial committee was set up composed of myself as chief editor – on that I insisted – Herbert Read and Gerhard Adler. In retrospect it did not make much difference; it was a pleasure to have Read there and Gerhard's function was defined as checking Hull's translations. On general policy there was virtual agreement. The work went forward relatively smoothly after I had arranged the content of Jung's volumes. However, there was a somewhat contentious editing by myself of *Psychology and Alchemy* (discussed further in Ch. 13).

During this time, soon after the war ended, I became involved in a project which brought me closer to Jung. There had been a society of mainly German psychiatrists and psychotherapists, the German Society for Psychotherapy, of which Professor Ernest Kretschmer had been president: he had also been the editor of the Society's journal. When the Nazis came to power, Kretschmer, because he was a Jew, resigned or was forced out of office, I do not know which. Jung was asked to accept the presidency and after some hesitation he did so, as long as the society was recognized as international. It acquired the cumbersome title of the International General Medical Society for Psychotherapy. New American, English, French and Dutch members joined, some of them asked to do so by Jung himself. His actions were resented, especially by psychoanalysts, who sometimes mounted a venomous attack on him. However, Jung remained at his post and made no serious defence until after the war, when he resigned and J.R. Rees, an English psychotherapist who had been a general during the war, took over and organized a conference with a committee of which I was member.

We began to receive attacks on Jung, some of them extremely offensive, and although the committee members did not appear to take much notice of them it was evidently up to me to defend him should it be necessary. As I knew next to nothing about it all, I wrote to Jung and received a clear answer about what he had done. But I wanted to talk with him face to face so I went out to Zurich. It will be remembered that I had heard a dissertation on the Jews when I first met Jung and could understand why some of what he said could be taken as anti-Semitic. I had not taken it like that for I could

understand his fascination with the Nazi movement as a manifestation of the collective unconscious. But I did not know Jung well at
the time so I was glad of the opportunity to make his further
acquaintance. My visit confirmed what I had thought. Jung was far
too much of a Swiss democrat and laid far too much emphasis on
the individual ever to have been an active Nazi collaborator. On this
occasion he told me that he had been on the Nazi blacklist, that his
books had been burned by the Germans in Paris and that he had
lodged a protest when the Germans wanted to organize a congress
during the war.

I also met other friends in Zurich and they told me that they had
implored Jung not to be so outspoken against the Nazis during the
war, and I talked to C.A. Meier, who had been secretary of the
society. He gave me details of Jung's visit of protest to Vienna where
the Germans were organizing a conference during the war, even
though many of the society's members would be debarred from
attending. He asserted that the Germans had no right to hold a
conference to an international society until the war was over. That
was a daring thing to do at the time. So, armed with a wealth of
ammunition to use if necessary, I returned to London. I never
needed to use what I had collected, owing to the sympathetic or
indifferent attitude of the committee's members.

Much later on I came across an example of what motivated Jung's
detractors. Dr Willie Hoffer, a psychoanalyst, wrote an article in the
Observer newspaper in which he attacked Jung and made a number
of statements which were manifestly untrue; so I wrote a letter in
reply which was duly printed. Now I knew Hoffer personally so I
asked him why he made statements that he must know were false.
'Oh', he said, 'I had a score to pay off' and he went on to tell me
that before the war he believed that, as a result of Jung's activities
in the International Society, one of his friends had been arrested by
the Gestapo and had been sent to a concentration camp, never to
be heard from again – a highly inflammatory statement! That gave
me an insight into why Jung was attacked so bitterly, especially by
psychoanalysts who had 'scores' to pay off from the past. It may be
remembered that Freud himself had believed Jung had anti-Semitic
tendencies. Jung would never have handed over a Jew to the
Gestapo, as Hoffer implied, and I know that Jung provided many

avenues of escape for Jews from Nazi Germany. There is no need to defend Jung, although at first he refused to defend himself on the grounds that it must all turn against his detractors in the long run. Later he took steps to explain his position in his book *Essays on Contemporary Events* (1947); I helped to facilitate the translation of that work.

Apart from this specific commitment to defend Jung if necessary whilst on the International Society's Committee in London, there was a constant stream of correspondence, often angry and resentful for one reason or another, and nothing to do with Jung, which made co-operation almost impossible. Eventually J.R. Rees decided to tour some of the more vociferous societies in various countries. So when some members of the SAP wanted me to stand for the Presidency of the new International Association for Analytical Psychology, I firmly declined, knowing that comparable conflicts would arise amongst Jungian analysts.

An activity that I enjoyed centred round the then Medical Section of the British Psychological Society. I joined its committee and worked with a number of prominent psychoanalysts, amongst whom I was especially impressed by John Rickman, Michael Balint and Clifford Scott. I came to know Rickman best and remember a delightful episode when Frieda and I were staying in her caravan on the shore of Lake Coniston in the Lake District. She had been left a horse-drawn caravan by her father and we spent many enjoyable holidays in it. One day a sailing boat came gently down the lake and I am not sure how it happened, but we found out that John Rickman was in it. He returned another day bringing fish, which Frieda cooked, and we enjoyed the fine weather, the good food and good company. Rickman had great charm and his warmth and sensitivity made him a delightful companion. It was mostly due to our relationship that the Section became a forum for discussions between psychoanalysts and analytical psychologists on such subjects as 'Archetypes and internal objects' and 'Counter-transference'.

In honour of Jung's seventieth birthday I wrote a paper: 'The development and status of Jung's researches'. It was published in the Medical Section's journal and C.A. Meier did me the honour of telling me that it was by far the best of the papers compiled for the occasion. Later I was asked to comment on Bion's 'Address from the chair', which I did; it was published as 'Reflections on individual and collective psychology'. I felt the paper was well received but I was astonished when Rickman came up and complimented me on its powerful effect, which I had not noticed at all. That made me aware of how little capacity I had, and still have, of judging the effect of a lecture on the audience. I think I become so absorbed in what I am trying to get across that I lose sight of its impact on the audience. Eventually I became chairman of the Medical Section and that gave access to the administrative functioning of the main Society. The chairman was required to attend Council meetings and I watched the operations of that august body with a mixture of awe and admiration. I became a member of the 'Committee on membership' where I devised a formula which allowed doctors to become members. I was also a member of a working party set up soon after the war which was drawing up a memorandum on delinquency for the Royal Commission on that subject.

I was, and still am, proud of being the first committed Jungian to become chairman of the Medical Section. It is true that E.A. Bennet, who supported many of Jung's ideas, had been in that office but he was then ambivalent, being always at pains to distinguish his position from any taint of 'Jungianism'. Later he committed himself fully and for a time was a member of the SAP. He was the only man I know to become a close friend of Jung, though a number of people have claimed that distinction! I owe to Bennet my appointment as consultant to the Child Guidance Clinic in what was then the West End Hospital for Nervous Diseases – it must have been in 1946. That was a very welcome appointment, for it meant that I could continue my work with children, which might otherwise not have been possible. He also proposed that I become assistant director which surprised me, for the clinic did not require a second director. But I thought that there could be no harm in accepting and I did so – I thought it might after all enhance my reputation abroad (I was thinking of Zurich in that connection). Dennis Newton, the real director, evidently felt shaken and he came to ask me whether I wanted to become director eventually. I could easily reassure him on that account. I had quite enough responsibility at the SAP, and together with the editing work it was enough. I assured him that I would be only too glad if he would continue with the administrative work. As to attendance at committees, we arranged that he would continue with that and I would only attend if he thought I could be useful. It was an arrangement which suited both of us and a happy collaboration continued until I retired. It was owing to this that I could continue with my study of autism, published in *The Self and Autism* (1976), and experiment with the team method current in child guidance.

For some time I had grown to think that the routine team procedure in which the psychologist tested the child, the psychiatric social worker interviewed his mother and a second interview with the child was conducted by the psychiatrist, followed by a conference to assess the material collected, was unnecessarily cumbersome. So I arranged for whatever members of the family came to the first interview to be seen by the psychiatric social worker and myself. An advantage of this procedure was that everybody knew what was going on and we could proceed from there. It was an interesting departure and it astonished me how nuclear family conflicts would display themselves almost at once. Sometimes the interview was repeated if an agreement as to what needed doing could not be arrived at with the family. I did not continue with family interviews or initiate family therapy since I held that psychotherapy was essentially a matter for individuals. So the procedure was adopted for diagnostic purposes: I and the psychiatric social worker endeavoured to assess who, if anybody, was motivated for psychotherapy so that our efforts could be most effectively engaged. If psychotherapy for the child was indicated we let it be known that help was available for parents if they needed it too, but we dispensed with routine interviews with parents. Indeed, if I was treating a child I would also arrange for interviews with the parents as well, thus starting to test whether the child therapist taking full responsibility for the case was a good way of proceeding. It proved both interesting and difficult but often worthwhile.

The other interest I was able to pursue was making long-term studies of a few cases of infantile autism. This was partly of theoretical interest: to test a theory that autism was a disorder of the self in which integration had taken on a pathological turn, so that what I termed deintegration, which brought the infant into relation with the environment, was disordered. In addition I suspected that the disorder, as described in the literature, was heterogeneous. I think this has now become recognized. My conclusions were first published in a French journal of psychiatry and the *British Journal of Medical Psychology* in 1966 and were subsequently published in *The Self and Autism*, with added experiences from other sources. I cannot say that this work had much impact and its reception was not encouraging. One case of secondary autism was, however, spectacularly successful; the child eventually achieved academic distinction at university and improved his social adaptation out of all recognition. Others I chose because I thought that the prognosis was not good and there was one who I thought was certainly not curable. Such analytic psychotherapy is sometimes said to be uneconomic, but all the children were looked after at home, thus saving the state the cost of providing for them in an institution. I do not think that the essential core of autism can be altered much by analytic means but many of the children who suffer from it can benefit significantly. One side-effect of these studies was that I confirmed the remarkable devotion that the children could often evoke in their mothers; sometimes that was evidently beneficial but sometimes I was less certain when the devotion was based on a delusion.

By now I had a rich and varied professional life and in addition there was the editing, which I will discuss later. It did not go forward smoothly, for almost at once Hull developed a severe attack of poliomyelitis and so the translation of *Psychology and Alchemy* was held up, since he could not do any work for a prolonged period. He began to improve, however, and the Bollingen Foundation helped both financially and with typing instruments. He gradually recovered enough to resume his translating. Unfortunately, he moved out of London and then to Switzerland, thus making it impossible to build up the closely-knit team that I was hoping for. Further difficulties arose over the translation of Greek and Roman texts, and Jung became worried by the long delay.

13   EDITING

Embarking on an occupation about which I knew very little was a formidable task. How formidable I was to discover as time went on. I had a very good idea of how Jung's works could be organized: the volumes would be arranged according to subject-matter, starting from his experimental studies and ending with his erudite investigations into religion and alchemy. The result had a chronological element but a subject had often continued to interest Jung over prolonged periods and consequently many volumes would contain matter which would disrupt a chronological sequence in the volumes. The whole conception had been preformed in my essay written for Jung's seventieth birthday celebrations. In principle it was a simple idea and I set down an arrangement which Jung, Read and Barret accepted. It was never significantly altered though the last volume (20) was expanded to include some matter, such as the 'Tavistock Lectures', which did not come strictly from Jung's own hand because it was an edited transcript. I was somewhat surprised that nobody raised the alternative idea of simply printing Jung's publications in strictly chronological order, as some scholars might have preferred.

I used Jolande Jacobi's bibliography to make a provisional arrangement of items, finding in the process omissions and errors such as would be expected in a first effort to assemble such a document. So I made journeys to Zurich after gaining permission to examine Jung's files. There I made contact with Miss Schmidt,

Jung's secretary, who was easy to collaborate with and a great help. We found many articles in English, French and German which expanded the bibliography considerably, and I brought back a number of offprints to London. It was a painstaking labour, at times quite exciting and, as it proved, well worthwhile in getting a better perspective on Jung's work.

Then came the question of which volume to publish first and the editors acceded to Jung's strongly felt wish that it be *Psychology and Alchemy*. It was never quite clear why he wanted it that way but it may be assumed that he wanted to introduce his work on alchemy soon, since although important volumes were out of print, much of his other work was already available in English. Examining that volume showed how complicated it was and I thought it was made more difficult by being interspersed with Greek and Latin texts which would prove incomprehensible to many readers, especially in the United States. I referred the matter to Read, who consulted a professor of his acquaintance, and Dr Wasserstein was deputed as a suitable translator. After some time a difficulty arose: neither he nor his professor could make sense of some of the Latin and Greek texts. They referred it to me and I suggested that a literal translation might be attempted and then we would go over the difficult parts together. If necessary we could consult somebody more conversant with the classical languages and subject-matter than I. I could not easily consult Hull who was in Switzerland, and I was disconcerted by his already having referred the matter to the Jungian analyst Marie Louise von Franz. She asserted that Wasserstein was making elementary mistakes in his translations. That I certainly did not believe but I consulted Adler and Read. For diplomatic reasons we decided to change translators and A.S.B. Glover was given the task, which he performed to everybody's satisfaction.

Glover was a professional editor and a delight to work with. His communications were always brief and to the point and often scribbled on odd bits of paper. He was tremendously erudite and had a formidable library with rooms and walls filled or covered with books of every kind. I do not know a lot about him but I found out that his whole body was tattooed including his left hand, on which he always wore a glove. He was a fund of amusing incidents such as the following: he was on the staff of Penguin Books and they decided to produce a book without fault: lo and behold it appeared with the title page upside down! He remarked that he was incapable of understanding how some printers' errors occurred, unless they threw the print on the floor and then attempted to put the fragments together from there. On another occasion he arrived at the front door with what appeared to be a large roll of toilet paper: it had a book written on it. Glover had been given it to edit and put into shape. That was the first time I had any intimation of the relation between writing and evacuation.

As a staunch rationalist Glover was incensed by Jung's long paper on synchronicity because it introduced an acausal connecting principle based on meaning. In the paper were some statistical data which Glover showed to a statistician, who pronounced that the data were nonsense and ought to be suppressed. Consternation ensued and the matter was referred to me. I enjoyed dealing with it, especially as it made me study elementary statistics and revived memories of student days when I enjoyed mathematics. All my labours had to be submitted to Jung and we had a lengthy correspondence about it, ending when he wrote: 'I hope this toing and froing can stop soon'. Fortunately that letter contained the answer to the last question I wanted to ask and there was no further letter-writing required on the subject.

It had been interesting for me but I do not think the alterations were especially important; it was more a diplomatic exercise to absorb the shock of the statistician's condemnation. I also came to understand a curious error that Jung had made when working on his astrological experiment. At one time he really thought that if his material proved statistically significant it would prove his thesis. Of course it was just the reverse, it would make a cause for the data more likely. I gained the impression that Jung did not like mathematics, and indeed in private he once said so. The job took me out to Zurich because I wanted to ascertain what kind of statistical method had been used by Professor Fiertz, the mathematician who had worked with Jung on the experiment. I thought that if the whole experiment was fallacious, the methods used were as important as the result. The meeting with him did not start off propitiously: Fiertz stonewalled about the experiment, indeed behaved as though he had got his fingers burned once and was not going to risk it again. Then I remembered that he had made mistakes in his calculations and Jung had announced that they were unconsciously motivated. He did, however, disclose that he had used the 'Poisson distribution'. In other respects the interview passed off amicably.

It was out of this study that I wrote my essay 'Reflections on the archetypes and synchronicity', which Jung praised most warmly in his 'Foreword' to my *New Developments in Analytical Psychology* (1957). There I introduced the idea that since Jung's data were not significant, they were not caused and that in as much as they came within the field of chance, they supported his thesis. He had evidently changed his mind about the meaning of statistical significance.

The delay in getting *Psychology and Alchemy* into print worried Jung quite a bit and matters were not helped by work on the galley proofs. These had been deemed necessary because of the complexity of inserting translations of Greek and Latin into the text and footnotes. The proofs were sent over on thin paper with too narrow margins for that purpose. I did my best but Bill McGuire, of the Bollingen Foundation, criticized my handling of them. It was to meet him and the staff of the Foundation that I was asked to go over to New York. The result was that since my plan of having a team all working in England had broken down owing to Hull's illness, McGuire became executive editor with a roving commission to liaise between the editors, Hull and the Zurich Jungians. He did all this with great skill and perseverance. Working with him revealed the remarkably high standards of his editorial activities, even if they were sometimes pedantic. I was also glad because the *Collected Works* were taking up much too much of my time, and to act in a supervisory capacity was more to my liking.

Another interesting episode arose from the editorial work. When it came to the chapter 'The type problem in poetry' in *Psychological Types*, Richard Hull wanted to restructure it so as to make the presentation more logical. I managed to show him that to do so would destroy the richness of Jung's writing. I take pride in having convinced him.

Editing the *Journal of Analytical Psychology* was a rather

different matter, partly because of the continual need to collect suitable papers and take a much more active part in defining policy and paying attention to administration. Therefore I insisted that if I took part in the work it would have to be as sole editor. There would be the usual assistant editors, but all decisions were to be mine. The alternative would have been a committee, but more committee work would have made my life unbearable – or so I thought. The parts of the work that I would enjoy most would be reading submitted manuscripts, corresponding with authors and grouping papers meaningfully – and so it proved. I had a clear idea of the policy to be pursued: it would be broadly based on the many-faceted shape of analytical psychology but special emphasis would be laid on work with patients. This would mean giving attention to methods used with patients and publishing case material, which would be opposed by influential analysts outside the London Society. The Journal was a project which I favoured, but it would not have started without Simon Stein, a speech therapist, who pushed hard and enthusiastically – I am not sure whether he was chairman of the SAP at the time. The Journal would certainly be a step forward in the maturation of the Society and a pioneering departure for analytical psychology. It was facilitated by a grant which I obtained through the good offices of Jack Barret, from the Bollingen Foundation.

I was friendly with C.A. Meier at the time and discussed the matter with him, pointing out that it was time such a journal was produced. He agreed and wanted it to be overtly international, as we did. He also wanted to be co-editor with me which neither I, nor our SAP members, wanted. They had become possessive: it was their journal and they did not want the Swiss muscling in on it. At a meeting in Zurich some of our members met Meier and a French analyst, Roland Cahen, and there was a good deal of animosity about our refusal to implement Meier's proposal. To my regret I was for some time estranged from Freddie Meier, who thought it was all my fault – the friendship was, I am glad to say, repaired later.

Another bone of contention was the title of the Journal. A number of analysts, especially in Switzerland, thought it ought to be called the *British Journal*. We stood to our guns, however: it would be the only Jungian journal in the world and we had initiated

it; once again the English were playing a pioneering role, were
proud of it and wanted recognition. I was somewhat apprehensive
lest the controversy alienated analysts from abroad. This did not
happen and among early contributors were Jung himself, Meier and
Jolande Jacobi, an analytical psychologist, from Switzerland; Joseph
Henderson and James Kirsch from the USA and Eric Neumann from
Israel. I had to work quite hard to get these articles. Among the
difficulties was an objection to our publishing Jung's article on the
grounds that it would diminish sales of the volume of the *Collected
Works* in which it was also due to appear. Jack Barret's counsel was
sought and he stated categorically that the reverse was true. That
settled the matter. To get the project going I solicited articles from
likely authors and suggested subject-matter. This is something that
some editors do not like doing unless they are very sure of the
quality of the product they will receive. I came unstuck only once.
I received an article which I had requested – it was so bad that I
could not publish it, nor could I see how it could be improved.
There was acrimony but I got away with it, although I knew that
the author could insist on publication. She did not do so.

There was much aggravation over a different problem: the agent
in the United States was, to put it mildly, unsatisfactory and even a
change in agent did not produce enough sales to make the Journal
financially viable. It was necessary to achieve that for the Bollingen
grant would not go on for ever. Eventually Harvard Watts of
Tavistock Publications told me that he thought we would do better
to publish the Journal ourselves. We took his advice and engaged
James Seddon and John Lucas, who performed the executive work
between them. Seddon in particular worked with great energy and
precision; it was largely due to his work that the circulation
increased sufficiently to continue publication.

After fifteen years as editor I retired. That had been long enough
and an injection of new blood was desirable. The Society gave me
a framed testimony of their appreciation which hangs on the wall
of my study today. Looking back on the period of my editorship, I
think that opposition had largely dispersed and the Journal had
developed a good enough reputation for respected persons to
publish in it. I would mention not only Jung, whose blessing was
essential, but also such non-Jungians as Arnold Toynbee the

historian, the psychologist A.C. Mace and the psychiatrist Aubrey Lewis. A lot had been achieved and I was proud of it.

I would like to end this segment of my reminiscences by mentioning the help of Alan Glover. After the Journal had been going for some time, I forget how long, I received a copy of it from Glover in which there were ninety corrections of various kinds. By now I knew what an experienced editor could do so I asked him why he troubled. It turned out that it was simply an offer of help and thereafter he did help without payment – he was an extraordinarily generous man.

Editing brought me a number of friends and interesting contacts, but I am not and never will be a real editor as it is understood by the Glovers and the McGuires of the literary world. From them I have acquired a critical stance towards book- and journal-production, but I do not have a pencil in my hand when reading a book or journal so that mistakes can be corrected as I go along, as Glover once told me he did. Editing produced appreciation of good book-production and all the work that went into it: the *Collected Works* was an example of that. I got satisfaction from witnessing the result; but once a book is produced my interest in it fades. That applies to my own creative work as well as that of others. My enjoyment of editing lay in the contribution I made, in the actual work. That applied especially to those occasions when in editing the Journal I was able to assist authors in improving the quality of their products. There was, I think, a background to my interest. At one time my father was interested in printing, possessed some books from William Morris's Caldicott Press, bound in vellum, and was closely associated with a press that produced fine books. The Bollingen series was the high point of good book-production and our Journal was good enough – in spite of its ninety errors in one issue!

As I have already mentioned Bill McGuire became a close friend. We enjoyed each other's company and provided each other with mutual hospitality. It was a sad day when his trips to Europe ended. I also became quite close to Richard Hull, but his rather Bohemian style of life and his habit of changing wives irked me. In addition I liked compressed communications (after Glover's style) whereas Hull's were lengthy – his letters went on for pages and pages! None the less he had a beautiful mind and his translations were a pleasure to read, even though they were sometimes criticized for 'improving' too much on the original Jung! It was also a privilege to know Herbert Read better and to enjoy his sensitive poetic nature. He also had a beautiful way of going straight to the point on editorial matters – his support was frequently invaluable. I should also mention Gerhard Adler who, of course, I knew before our collaboration in editing began. It was rumoured that I could not work with him but that was not the case. The truth was that I could and did work with him but I was not a friend of his. Not only was there a clear definition in our fields of operation in that he was to check on the accuracy of Hull's translations and made numerous journeys to Ascona to do so, but also because we found ourselves in almost complete agreement as to policy. When Adler was added to the editorial board Jung remarked that it would save me from learning German. All the same I made some rather fruitless efforts to do so.

14 JUNG

My debt to Jung is so great that I hardly dare to write about him. I have done so on another occasion and have been dissatisfied with what I produced. At the time, after his death in 1960, I found the idealization unbearable, although it is a natural part of mourning. Idealization pays little attention to the person subjected to that process and I tried to counterbalance the trend. To some extent that distorted my efforts, giving a wrong impression of my relationship with him. I did not convey my great respect and admiration but rather emphasized his faults and indiscretions. To me they were seldom offensive and usually amusing or even endearing. Like anybody else he had a shadow and his great stature did not absolve him of it. There was, in my mind, a strong association between Jung and my father, who also talked without regard for others, and who would also say outrageous things from time to time. He too was a striking character, could be very outspoken, and was also a creative man. Thus it was easy for Jung to take on a paternal role for me.

I cannot say that my first meeting with Jung was particularly auspicious. I have described that already but there are some further points I would like to make. In that first interview he seemed to be drawing a picture of parasitic elements in Jewish psychology but in a curious way that was not meant to demean them. He asked, 'What were they feeding on during the forty years they were in the desert?' A rhetorical question which left me to infer that they were grazing on the lands round the desert owned by other tribes until they were moved on. Then there was the statement that they were not the same as other races, and when Jung asserted that they might be wearing different clothes so as to emphasize the fact, I did not find this at all outrageous, just bewildering, for I understood he was speaking out of the unconscious where everything is concrete.

Then there was his lack of consideration. After all I had not come out to be harangued about the Jews. Yet it was all singularly familiar and I quickly grasped that he was possessed, like my father, who also used to talk outrageously when he was germinating ideas. My interview came at a time when Jung was intensely interested in the Nazi uprising and moved by it, but I am not sure whether he was being attacked then for having Nazi sympathies and consequent anti-Semitism (although Freud and other psychoanalysts had long suspected and even accused him of anti-Semitism). On that subject both he and I knew that Jews can bring prosperity to the countries they live in and are bearers of culture and learning. I got the strong impression that he had been deeply moved by what was going on in Germany and was struggling after objectivity and understanding, using his theory of the collective unconscious and the archetypes to do so. After all, I reflected, European nations had characteristics that were different from others so why not the Jews also? As to the clothes, variations in dress between European nations are minimal but Arabs, Indians and Chinese all dressed differently. So I did not understand his diatribe as anti-Semitic; subsequently I came to know how many Jews he numbered amongst his students and how loyal and supportive he was to them.

There was another element that made for some confusion in my mind, which would go some way towards explaining his discourse. I had learned that Jung had an astonishing intuition so I asked myself whether he was, in some sense, delivering a message to me. I had also heard that he would talk directly out of the unconscious and in that case he might have seen me as, like the Jew, wanting to migrate into Switzerland and live off the Swiss, that is, he was, by indirect methods, drawing my attention to my shadow. This is all somewhat fantastic but those were the kind of thoughts I had to wrestle with at the time. Much of it was an unanalysed transference but some of it made sense. Over and above all that there was something else which I could not define, though it came from Jung himself. I cannot see that it makes any rational sense but much of my relation to Jung fits into place when I understand that I loved him after the episode in Zurich, like I loved my father. Ever after he seemed especially kind in a very agreeable and intimate way. He gave ample evidence of his good opinion of me and it was after all he who suggested that I become editor of his *Collected Works*. He was always accessible when I wanted to see him, whilst his letters were, with one or two exceptions, perceptive and ended with 'cordially'.

As a consequence of my visit to Zurich I could not get analysis from Jung. In retrospect I am glad that I never trained in Zurich but took in as much as I needed in visits and through my personal relation with Jung himself and others, amongst whom I would mention Freddie Meier, the analytical psychologist Barbara Hannah and, later, Jolande Jacobi. I next met Jung when he came to deliver the Tavistock Lectures. Then I listened with admiration to his masterly presentation.

It must have been in 1936 when Jung lectured at St Bartholomew's Hospital that, because of my difficulties with Baynes, I asked for and was given a personal interview, the one mentioned earlier that was held in his bedroom whilst he was changing for dinner. I don't think I would have made the change of analyst from Baynes to Hilde Kirsch without Jung knowing about it because I needed his objectivity. I especially liked the informality of the interview. It expressed something about Jung that I met afterwards – a disregard for formality and a direct and open approach – no sign of beating about the bush. There were no obstructions to my need for a change of analyst nor to my positive transference to Hilde. He did remark, however, that I should know that Hilde and James (her husband) would use my material against Baynes. My feeling about that was clear: I did not conceive that to be my business. I wanted an analyst who would relate to me and to a large extent that is what Hilde did.

I would like to comment further on Jung's informality and formality. He seemed to function in two ways: one was formal and that was more in evidence when at Kusnacht (I am not referring to the delightful dinner or lunch meetings when Emma Jung and Frieda were also present); the other was more personal and

Mrs Jung

Photo: Dora Bernhard

informal, exhibited best out at his Bollingen house when one usually sat with him beside the lake on a stone bench with one of his stone carvings nearby.

It was when Frieda and I had a meal with the Jungs that we started to make Emma's acquaintance. Both of us liked her and were impressed by her. She was not at first very communicative because her husband tended to take the stage, but she contributed to the conversation in a perceptive and sometimes penetrating way. It was clear that she very much had a mind of her own which was appreciative of but not subservient to that of her husband. Later on Frieda stayed at Kusnacht and I, on a different occasion, went to Emma for a few analytic interviews, and our impression of her was amply confirmed. She made important contributions to analytical psychology, especially in giving the animus a far more favourable function as the basis for the logos function in a woman. She also wrote a study of the Grail symbolism which was never published but was swallowed by Marie Louise von Franz, who made it into a book of her own in which Emma's contribution was destroyed. This was done at Jung's instigation and he will not be forgiven by me for it. Emma was a careful student of the subject, both down to earth and interesting.

Working with Jung over his *Collected Works* was entirely agreeable: he left one very much alone to get on with the job but was open and responsive when I approached him with some problem. There were occasions when he could have been irritated or angry, but he was not. Most of the work was conducted by correspondence, though I went over to Zurich from time to time: at least once a year and sometimes more. He was very even-tempered, although as I have shown he could be very outspoken and cause offence. It so happens that I liked his outspokenness because it was usually apt. I was familiar with it in my father and myself, but there was no sign of it during the editing.

In another context, however, he made me very angry: a burglar had invaded St Katherine's Precinct in London and had hit Frieda on the head with a metal instrument, causing a depressed fracture of the skull. The man, whom I caught and handed over to the police, was tested by a student of mine and found to be a mentally defective epileptic. When I told Jung about the incident he started to talk about how such people sometimes brought a message. That kind of approach, however correct or incorrect, lacked sensitivity and was not on as far as I was concerned. It was made worse in that I knew of his interest in mental defects. Cretins were at one time conceived to be good Christians (*bon Chrétien*), but I did not want another lecture on the subject just then. I think he saw how angry I was for he shut up and we spoke of other things.

Here is another example of how he could be outspoken and cause pain. Herbert Read was to give a long paper in two parts at the Eranos meeting in Switzerland. I did not go to the first part but was coming to the second. There was a sloping path down to the lecture hall and as I came to the top of it I heard a man shouting and cursing at the entrance to the flat in which Jung and Emma lived during the *Tagung* – it was above the lecture hall. I went and spoke to the man, who was Jung himself! He was angry with his wife for having 'stolen' the key to their flat, but that did not last long and he went into a tirade against Read who was lecturing on Picasso, of whom, it appeared, Jung had a very low opinion. After he had gone on for a bit I intervened to point out that Read was a writer and an aesthete and could not be expected to grasp Picasso's psychological significance in the way Jung was able to do. I cannot remember details of the conversation but Jung was mollified and we were soon laughing and joking and I went on down to the lecture. Later I met Read, who was standing on his own shyly shifting from one foot to another, quite unlike his usual self – it was clear that he had been very much hurt. Subsequently I learned what had happened: before the lecture there had been a dinner party and Jung had sat next to Read, who told him he was going to talk about Picasso. That had upset Jung and he made derogatory remarks about the artist. Worse was to come because Jung thought Read did not make it clear when he was quoting from Jung and when he was not, so Jung started shouting out during the lecture: 'That's me' or 'That's not me'. Whether he walked out before the end of Part One or left at its ending, I do not know, but he was certainly not there for Part Two.

Jung was aware of this tendency which was a kind of roughness, often witty, biting and sometimes brutal. I found this out when I commented on it and asked him about it. It got him into trouble, he said, and gave an instance of it: at a banquet in Germany he was asked about the large swastika hanging on the wall. He replied that as a symbol it went the wrong way round! He added that a friend got him out of trouble by saying that what Jung had said was true if you looked at it from the outside only, but what if you were inside it? The tense atmosphere was dispersed.

My personal relationship with him made me aware of a trend amongst some of his followers, and his detractors as well, which he deplored. It hinted that analytical psychology was a sort of religion. It was an error that I also deplored, and so I gave lectures and wrote papers to oppose the tendency. One, on the mysticism of St John of the Cross, was written for a Festschrift on Jung's seventieth birthday and was published in Switzerland; others were delivered to the Guild of Pastoral Psychology in England.

That was one prong to my activities which brought me into closer relation with Jung. The other was my interest in developing a theory of infant and child development. Jung had the germ of such a theory but he lacked the necessary experience, which I had. From time to time I tried to interest him, but my efforts never had much success even though he gave a seminar on children's dreams. One day when we were having lunch I made a renewed effort, but he would only concede that the dreams of children were scientifically interesting, but as for child psychotherapy, if a child was brought to him he 'got the mother by the ears'. He went on in this vein until Emma broke in: 'You know very well that you are not interested in anybody unless they exhibit archetypes!' and that was the end of the matter for quite a time. Emma was a good ally of mine in this work. I realize that my account of what happened does not make sense, for Jung had said elsewhere that children's dreams were so interesting just because of their archetypal content. That, however is how I remember it – Frieda had a somewhat different version, though the sense was the same. Yet as far as I observed, Jung had a quick and quite delightful capacity to relate to children. There were his grandchildren out at Bollingen: they seemed so happy enjoying themselves outside the house in a copse, although I did notice that the entrance door was locked, when I was there anyway. On one occasion I took Max to see him at Kusnacht. He made easy contact with him at once when I introduced them to each other.

Another of my interests was the transference, and this deepened my relationship with Jung. I had found that the analysts claiming to have been trained in Zurich did not know how to handle it or sometimes even recognize its existence. Yet Jung wrote interestingly on the subject and had been positively lavish in his praise for my article 'Notes on the transference' (published in *New Developments in Analytical Psychology* in 1957). I became increasingly puzzled and decided I must do something about it. I did not confront him with my somewhat paranoid fury, I did not accuse him directly of saying one thing and practising another but I waited until I had a dream about it, which I presented to him. He analysed it carefully and methodically and as he did so I was able to distinguish the pathological parts of my rage and see that he understood my transference projections without, however, mentioning them. My not altogether rational conclusion was that Jung had created a situation in which I could do this. The analysis proceeded until he came to the figure of Heracles at the end of the hour. Then he seemed to leap out of his chair with a loud exclamation and insisted we had another meeting 'tomorrow'. But the second meeting was no good. I had accomplished my heroic task in the first and that was all I needed to do. I returned to England convinced that he might not handle the transference as we were trying to do in England, but he knew how to digest it and feed it back to me. Whether that was conscious or not basically did not matter.

I have thought a lot about that interview. It showed, once again, how if Jung got on the track of an archetype he tended to lose sight of the person in whom it was active. At one time I thought that the second interview was pointless. It certainly revealed nothing new and we did not refer to Heracles, but its sheer unproductiveness made him ordinary again. Perhaps he was conforming with standard practice not to interpret the transference when only a few interviews are possible. Another fact is that unconscious action can be much more important than words and so on. There were many uncertainties, but the effect was decisive.

I mention these two activities of mine (emphasis on the

transference and the possibilities of child analysis) because I have come across resistances to them from other Jungian analysts. It is argued that I had even ceased to be a Jungian altogether. It will be clear that in my view that has not been the case. Moreover, Jung knew about these interests and, although we might disagree about child analysis, he seemed quite happy with disagreement and was instrumental in starting Dora Kalff on her sand tray method of treating children, as was Emma Jung also. It was she who introduced Dora Kalff to me and I introduced her to Margaret Lowenfeld. So he could agree to that kind of treatment, although I suspect he was more interested in the display of archetypal imagery which the method often evoked.

I have picked out striking events in my relation with Jung but once the editing started there were, besides the annual editorial meeting, lunch and dinner parties and private meetings. These were either at Kusnacht, to which Frieda also came if she was in Zurich, and they were all most enjoyable and relaxed, often sitting out in the garden by the lake; or out at Bollingen where the informality was especially delightful. It was these meetings over the years that consolidated the goodness of the relationship. I believe that I was, if not the last visitor to Kusnacht, very nearly so, before Jung's death. The visit came about as follows: a member of the Analytical Psychology Club in England brought me a letter he had received from Jung about which he was distressed. It was written in very shaky hand-writing and was an account of how he felt he had failed in his mission – he was misunderstood and misrepresented.

Now before his death my own father had been in a similar state of mind and I had been unable to help him and so I wanted to do something for Jung which I had not been able to do for my father. Therefore I went out to Zurich in 1960 only to hear that Jung was too ill to see anybody. I rang his house and Miss Bailey, who looked after Jung after Emma's death, answered the phone. She said that he was in a bad state but told me I should come along – 'It would do him good'. When I arrived he was in his dressing-gown looking very frail. I told him about the letter and how distressed I was about it. I then went on to say how we in England were in a strong position to rebut open misunderstandings and were striving to further recognition of his work. As I talked I started to realize that Jung did not want to hear such reassurances. He seemed to become weaker and weaker, looking at me as if I were a poor fool who did not know a thing. He did not reply but, after a short time, he rose from his chair and I thought he was going to have a fit. All he said was: 'Fordham, you had better go' and I walked out of the room feeling sad and a failure. I think he died, if not the next day, at least in the next few days. I have had no heart to go out to Zurich since his death, though Frieda and I went to his funeral.

I have pondered over that look which he gave followed by his dismissing me. Jung had a very good idea of his worth and of the importance of his work, not only in individual therapy but also for the future of mankind. That had been shown in various of his publications: there was his vision of the coming disaster after the First World War; his understanding that the German problem was not ended by it and his anticipation of a second holocaust and his interpretation of it when it arose. Then there were his studies of Christianity, his book *Answer to Job* and his welcoming of the Assumption of the Virgin by the Pope. All these were important to him as indicating the urgent need for man to become conscious of his own nature, sometimes expressed as the coming of the new man, which was necessary if humanity was to survive its own achievements. It may have been these profound matters that had made him feel that he had not succeeded in his mission. When I came to see him I did not touch on these matters but spoke superficially. If I had not done that I would have had to convey my thought that it was the delusion of being a world saviour that made him feel a failure – I had not the stature to do that.

15 Journey to the United States

After the editing of the *Collected Works* had continued slowly for some time, partly because it had run into difficulties, Jack Barret invited me to go over to New York and give a progress report, and I was very glad to do so. Once there I renewed my acquaintance with him and his efficient secretary, Jean Gilmore. After a discussion at the Bollingen Foundation, I was generously entertained by Jack in his New York house by the river: it had an old-world atmosphere reminding me of Georgian houses in England. There was a butler and beautiful furniture, French in style. He later invited me to a second, single storey house in Maine, which he had converted: it sounded as if he had just taken a suitable instrument and, in no time at all, cut off the upper floors. Apart from that, the meal was served by a maid dressed up to perform the part – not since my childhood had I enjoyed such elegance!

A most important event was meeting Bill McGuire. In contrast to Barret, Bill lived in what seemed to be a slum. When I went to see him there were some seemingly adolescent young men sitting on the steps up to the flat – they were not at all willing to let me pass, though after some parley they did so. When I told Bill and his wife about this there was some alarm and hopes that I had not offended them. It appeared that they were a gang and if offended would come and smash up the flat! Nothing happened, I am glad to say. It was a glance at the shadow of New York, of which there was further evidence in men lying out on the street who, I learned, were the 'bums', and were drunk on methyl alcohol. We met them later in a bar to which Bill took me at my request. It was all rather horrific: a large space with a fat woman, bawling her head off to the accompaniment of a somewhat debilitated piano. The 'bums' were let in as a side-show: they came along and threatened us if we did not give them money. If they became too menacing, a man came and moved them off to my – if not to Bill's wife and another guest's – relief. The episode in the bar occurred after we had gone to see a play about the English group of writers in Berlin before the war. It was fascinating because I had known some of them and the performance was excellent. I learned from Bill that Auden was now living in New York and his violent drunken parties were well known. I did not attempt to meet him again since I had not made any contact with him since school days.

It was at this time that a friendship with Bill began, beyond the editorial work we did together. It was through him that I learned what a professional editor was like. I got to know Bill's meticulous and scholarly work in detail, not to mention his diplomatic skills. A good example of his work was the bibliography of Jung's publications. A start had been made by Jolande Jacobi and I had developed it into a pamphlet; eventually it grew into a whole volume which was incorporated into the *Collected Works*.

I also met some of the analysts in New York. I had never met Esther Harding, who with Eleanor Bertine had formed an exclusive unit of Jungians centring round the Analytical Psychology Club in New York. She was said to be a benevolent and mostly well-loved dictator, who insisted that anybody who wanted to join the group had to submit to analytic contacts with her. I had also heard that she was hostile to the analytic study of childhood, because the analysis of childhood would provide a defence against working on the serious problems of adult persons pursuing the mature task of individuation. Yet when I gave a lecture on an archetypal dream of a small girl, with amplifications of ethnological material, it was better received than I expected, perhaps because I said nothing about child analysis. I found the audience well-informed and intelligent.

After New York I went on to San Francisco where, thanks to the good offices of Joseph Wheelwright, I had been invited to give lectures and seminars about children. It was all an enjoyable and instructive experience: there was no objection to child analysis but nobody practised it and did not do so till many years later. I suppose that was due to the resistance to it – said to emanate from Jung himself – among Jungians. I stayed with Joe and Jane in their house at Kenfield and lectured mostly in the evenings, although my address at the Langley Porter Clinic was delivered during the morning. I also attended a clinic at Stanford University where I listened to a psychiatric social worker giving a beautiful account of an 'intake interview'. The subsequent discussion was along psychoanalytic lines, to which Joe also contributed in a psychoanalytic fashion. This illustrated my friend's contention that Jungian and Freudian disciplines were not divorced, as in New York.

Before going over to the States, knowing I would be giving a number of lectures, I had been studying work on the attention span of audiences. I had learned that after forty minutes the audience began to relax and after fifty minutes not much could be assimilated at all, so I gave a public lecture lasting about fifty minutes. At the end of a lively discussion Joe came up to me and told me that my lecture had been much too short: 'You can't do that', he said, 'they don't get their money's worth!' So next time I went on for an hour and a half. To my surprise some very intelligent and perceptive comments and questions came from the last part of my lecture – most of them from Gregory Bateson, who could hardly be called an average listener! In free time there was sightseeing and other enjoyable pursuits.

Next I went on to Santa Barbara where I was told that being an introvert I would need to meditate before the lecture, but first came tea, when I was introduced to members of the Jungian group. Then I was sent to a small room to do what I ought, though I don't remember meditating. I had been told that there was interest in the role of the father and the place of discipline in bringing up children. It was a question promoted by the enthusiasm for permissive upbringing. After the lecture there was a large and lavish dinner party – it went on into the early hours of the morning. The children attending it looked more and more bedraggled and exhausted. Nobody, let alone a parent, thought of relieving them of their boredom by taking them off to bed so that they could go to sleep. Not a good advertisement for permissive upbringing, I thought.

Early next morning, at breakfast, I was made to answer questions and engage in discussion before I went on to join Joe and Jane. They took me on to Jane's brother's house further down the coast. Luxury again, and in addition I was given some interesting observations on infants by Jane's brother, who was a paediatrician. We then went on an excursion across the desert to stay with some friends near the Mexican border, getting a taste of Mexico in a restaurant in a cave across the border. I had never been near a desert before and the miles and miles of sand and the heat created an indelible impression. We spent the night in a motel and then there was more sand until large piles of rock began to dot the scene – they seemed like small hills with almost vertical sides. There was more luxury and a meal across the Mexican border.

I travelled to Los Angeles on a transcontinental train, to my great delight, even though it was a night-time journey. I have always liked trains and train journeys. A small compartment was provided to sleep in and there was a large observation car at the back in which film stars were showing themselves off. In Los Angeles there was a similar round of lectures and meetings to that in San Francisco, but run with a markedly different idea of what was valuable in Jung's work. Far more reliance was placed on its irrationality, so that there was an esoteric flavour to it all. The Society of Jungian Analysts of Southern California was being built up by James and Hilde Kirsch, who had migrated from England where I had been Hilde's patient. I can illustrate the difference between Los Angeles and San Francisco by saying that in the former horoscopes and the I Ching worked wonders, in the latter miracles were not on. Consequently the two groups were not on good terms, to put it mildly, and Joe Wheelwright spoke forcefully about some of the clinical practices of the Los Angeles group!

In Los Angeles I received the same warm welcome and generosity as I had met elsewhere on my journeys; I also had some contact with UCLA. This was not due to the enterprise of James or Hilde Kirsch but to Bruno Klopfer, who was a professor of psychology there. His special interest in projective techniques had led to collaboration with Jung in producing the Rorschach test. It was a most exciting evening when I spoke at the university. There was a good-sized hall with comfortable armchairs where there would have been benches in an English university. The audience was large and the discussion was alive and penetrating. It went on for a long time until somebody, I think it was Bruno Klopfer, stopped it on the grounds that I must be exhausted. I had not thought so, indeed, I found it most invigorating. Nevertheless, afterwards I realized that I had been stretched to the limit.

Next morning I took the flight back to New York. On the trip the plane circled round the Grand Canyon, a glorious and impressive sight. The flight took up nearly the whole day. I stayed a few nights with Violet de Laszlo, an analytical psychologist whom I had known when she was in England, and then took the long transatlantic flight home. In the morning we arrived over the tip of Ireland and the captain announced that in three-quarters of an hour the plane would be landing at Heathrow! I was quite shattered to think of the size of the United States and the smallness of England.

That was the first of several excursions to the States. I had made quite a close relation with analysts in San Francisco and Los Angeles, where both were interested in work with children and the child in adult patients. However, in both cities it was years before anybody started to practise child therapy, let alone analysis; a training in child therapy was first instigated in Los Angeles, at the behest of Hilde Kirsch. My journey marked a turning point in my professional life in that my position as a respected analytical psychologist was established, not only in England, but also abroad as well. Much of this was due to my own exertions, but it would not have been possible without the inspiration provided by Jung; whilst Frieda gave me a sense of partnership and security which I had not felt since my mother's death.

Reading through what I have written I see that I have given impressions of analytical psychology in the States, and I will conclude with further reflections. My excursions had made me more impressed with the country – its vast dimensions, the friendliness of its inhabitants – than with analytical psychology, since most of what I found I already knew about. There was the original work by Esther Harding, published as *Woman's Mysteries* as well as large volumes on *Psychic Energy* and another one on

Bunyan as an exemplar of individuation, *Journey into Self*. In San Francisco Joe Wheelwright had combined with Grey, a psychologist, to start experimental work on types and Wheelwright used type theory intensively in his practice; Joseph Henderson, a leading analytical psychologist in San Francisco, was developing his ideas, especially about initiation; in Los Angeles James Kirsch was working on a theory that there was a religious layer to the collective unconscious and studying the Bible and Shakespeare. Finally, Bruno Klopfer developed his own group to study projective tests. Only in San Francisco was there the beginning of an attempt to train analysts. The other two groups in New York and Los Angeles were, it seemed, relying more on the vocational idea with its absolute dependence on dreams and active imagination. I suspected that New York analysts had to have Esther Harding's agreement before they were accepted. Prospective analysts in Los Angeles had to go out to Zurich for a protracted period of study.

16 THE SOCIETY OF ANALYTICAL PSYCHOLOGY

The Society of Analytical Psychology in London remained the main centre of my interest and attention for many years. It grew quite rapidly since a number of men and women wanted to take our training. They were an interesting group, coming from the three disciplines we had decided to accept as a preliminary qualification: doctors, psychologists and psychiatric social workers. All of them had worked with psychoanalysts or Jungians. The more active, and even forceful, members of the training group were psychiatrists who had been in the army and had other experience in clinics and mental hospitals. Some of them came from the Maudsley teaching hospital where E.A. Bennet was on the staff, expounding Jung's psychological concepts and supervising clinical work with cases. Our choice of trainees was, I think determined by what groups of professional persons would be interested in improving their understanding of patients and developing techniques for dealing with them. It was also thought that these people would be the most likely to find Jung's knowledge useful. It turned out that they exerted a decisive influence on the way the Society developed.

At first our training programme was skeletal but it was enough to keep the trainees interested, although a few thought they already knew what we had to say and took the view that they had their own contribution to make. On the whole they provided quite valuable criticism. I do not remember the details of the seminars but they covered psychological types, the theory of archetypes (the shadow, the anima and animus) and the self. As I now recollect the teaching did not meet sufficiently the students' practical requirements because 1) its clinical orientation was insufficiently rigorous and 2) it did not convey the inspirational element in Jung's work. A particular need was for a theory of analytical practice, and that we did not have, and there was resistance by the Zurich-trained analysts to creating one. They were wedded to the doctrine of the closed vessel. They believed that the relation between analyst and patient was sacrosanct, and detailed discussion of it was felt to be almost a heresy. In addition, senior analysts were unwilling to give details about the analysis of their candidates and wanted only to give judgements on their merits. So enquiry into what analysts did came up against resistances and later open obstruction. No theory of practice is worth the paper it is written on unless it is related to what analysts do, so some of us started to give the matter serious thought.

I supported the new analysts, having previously become convinced that the Zurich ones were dangerously ignorant of the transference and countertransference, about which I and others had gained information from psychoanalysts and our child and adult patients. Jung's concept was of an almost chemical interaction between analyst and patient so it seemed possible to build on that, thus avoiding 'heresy'. Eventually I formulated the syntonic countertransference in which the analyst unconsciously introjected the patient's conflict. In order to become conscious of it the analyst had, therefore, to examine himself to find an element alien to himself but applicable to his patient. I was successful in interesting analysts in my idea, which I published as 'Notes on the transference' in my book *New Developments in Analytical Psychology*. Jung agreed to write an introduction and I was quite overcome by his praise of my chapter on transference. I had defined the differences between Jung and myself in that chapter, but Jung told me that I had exaggerated them and he did not think they were as great as I made out.

I would here like to say that though I am frequently thought to have been the originator of the conception of syntonic counter-transference, other members of the society were thinking along the same lines, although I did invent the term. Robert Moody in particular wrote a beautiful short paper on his countertransference to a child in which he described what I had named. Fred Plaut had also written on incarnating the animus. None the less, I thought I had made a new discovery at the time and was somewhat chagrined to find that the psychoanalyst Paula Heimann had written about the same phenomenon some years before I had written anything. Since some of our members and I were working with psychoanalysts, I think it quite likely that their ideas had been instrumental in forming our own.

As time went on the ideas and practices of our analysts gradually became a matter of concern. To make up for our deficiencies we had taken in bits of psychoanalytic technique and tried to assimilate them with varying success. In addition, lack of interest in the Zurich point of view was serious and eventually led to an identity crisis. Few of our trainees had been out to Switzerland. So, to give them a taste of what it was like, I induced some of the better-known analysts there to come over and give us their viewpoint in seminars. The first was Marie Louise von Franz, who talked to us on her brilliant study of fairy tales: later Barbara Hannah, Riwkah Scharf, Freddie Meier and Jolande Jacobi all made an attempt to interest our members. But our members thought they were clinically naive and exhibited a derogatory and critical attitude, which created a bad atmosphere. Scharf in particular stated, in private, that she was the authority and her work was beyond criticism. It was fortunate that Freddie Meier stood up to the attack and hit back effectively, whilst Mrs Jacobi, speaking on homosexuality, rather enjoyed the hurly-burly. When Esther Harding, the very determined 'Jungian' from New York, arrived I was determined to keep order so I took the chair. The evening went off without disturbance.

So the result of my first effort to establish a relation with Zurich was not a success and thereafter no analysts came over nor were they invited. They lectured to the Analytical Psychology Club, which is not a professional organization but a diverse group of people interested in Jung's work. However, there was some interest in Zurich in what we were doing and Toni Frey, then a budding analyst, came over to take our training. Mario Jacobi, a student of Jolande Jacobi, also came over and I had quite detailed discussions with him. By contrast I gave a number of lectures on children at the

Zurich Institute which attracted large audiences, but it was Frieda who made a breakthrough with her sensitive clinical lecture on her treatment of a patient. It evoked quite widespread admiration and since then a number of our analysts have been invited to address members of the Institute in Zurich.

I think it is relevant here to reprise a few remarks on why my published clinical material has been largely about children. Partly I wanted to interest Jungians in them but also most of my more interesting adult patients were potential analysts and so might be too easily identified. There was also, I now think, an unconscious reaction deriving from my material having been published by Baynes.

As the students became analysts and took seminars of new students, I became quite alarmed at their orientation – too little attention was given to Jung's work. So I gave a seminar on mythology, hoping to interest them in Jung's use of myths. Those seminars were wrongly focused, were not appreciated and were not repeated. I gave another on Jung's essay 'Psychology of the transference' with some trepidation, since it required an introduction to alchemical experience. One student offered to report on that complex document: her report was masterly and so impressive that I could add nothing to what she had said, nor could any of the students. So at least one student knew a lot about Jung. That student subsequently became a vigorous contributor to our deliberations of a child analytic training that was under consideration at the time. Sadly, she departed to Canada but before going she delivered a withering attack on some dream seminars given by Vera von der Heydt at the end-of-term meeting of students and seminar leaders. It was too hard for Vera to take and she never gave another seminar. The attack voiced a view taken by some – probably the majority – of the students. It was not only Vera who came under criticism, for one of my students told me of her boredom in one of my seminars on the grounds that 'you were so Jungian', and Gerhard Adler complained that the students went to sleep in his seminar! They did not want to hear about the seemingly more esoteric aspects of Jung's work and wanted more information that would facilitate their treatment of patients. As the Zurich analysts could not get their message across we had to get along as best we could, and as my interest was mainly clinical – that is to say, I was interested in what patients had to tell me and how I responded – I could not conceal my support for the attitude displayed by the trainees.

That formed the basis for what came to be called the London School of Analytical Psychology. It was said to be anti-Jungian and much too psychoanalytic. Subsequently we were told that we were a manifestation of the English school of empirical philosophy. For my part I had been struck by how little regard the 'Zurich Jungians' paid to Jung's firm claims that he was an empirical scientist himself and that he included psychoanalysis amongst the tools which a psychotherapist was required to use. However, the criticisms led me to glance at the philosophies of Locke and Hume, which I had never studied before, but I soon gave up since they did not seem to me of much relevance. If I wanted to understand them in philosophical terms it would have involved too much work. In addition I did not think the supposed reproach was made out of knowledge of the subject; furthermore, I could not see that trying to solve the highly emotional conflict could be resolved by removing it into the realms of abstract thought.

One difficulty of members, who felt they were developing Jung's science and communicating their ideas, was to understand the attacks made on them at the first conference held by the International Association for Analytical Psychology: their ideas and clinical findings came across vigorous resistance. A paper by Murray Jackson on symbolism focused the conflict. He introduced the idea that a useful distinction was to be made between symbolic equations and symbolic representations – a Kleinian idea put forward by Hanna Segal. His paper was discussed unfavourably by Esther Harding who, in a private conversation, wanted to fix the meaning of the term symbol, so that the Jungian meaning could not be altered as Murray Jackson had done.

My own position in all this was difficult. I knew that my interest in applying Jung's thesis to childhood would evoke criticism and that it would become worse as I applied my findings to the adult patients. I had published my investigations into childhood in *The Life of Childhood* and also in *New Developments in Analytical Psychology*, but also there was *The Objective Psyche* (1958), in which I collected together a number of essays expounding Jung's position to various audiences, most importantly to the Medical Section of the British Psychological Society. These were much more Jungian in the 'classical' sense than were my other investigations. I thought when that book came out: 'Well, my opponents will not be able to say that I have not studied Jung'. It was a curious reflection since I was on good terms with Jung and by that time had become editor of his *Collected Works*. He had not objected to my investigation of children's psychology and had praised the essays on transference, not to mention others of my writings. I do not know that *The Objective Psyche* had much effect but I had the satisfaction of knowing that Jung had recommended it to one of his pupils, a cleric, and had written warmly about the essay of the same title as the book.

The book, which did not sell well and was eventually remaindered, contained a number of papers on the psychology of religion. I wanted to check the tendency to exclusiveness, religiosity and cult formation. As mentioned, I had the impression that Jung did not like the tendency any more than I did. I admired Jung's researches in the religious field but thought that they were being misused. At this time I became fascinated by *The Dark Night of the Soul*, a tract written by the Spanish mystic St John of the Cross, and had contrasted the scientific with the religious approach: the former took the mystical expediences as a manifestation of the human psyche, the latter conceived it to be a transcendent experience of God himself. A Catholic theologian had taken exception to my ideas and we had a vigorous discussion in which he displayed as much ignorance of psychology as he contended I had of mysticism. I also knew Victor White, a Catholic priest who had been to study with Jung, quite well and staged a more fruitful discussion in our Journal. Kenneth Lambert, who had been a priest and was now one of our analysts, also took part in it.

Thus, in what might be called the post-war period, I was fighting battles on several fronts: within the Jungian fold and outside it in the British Psychological Society, the Guild of Pastoral Psychology and another society I have not mentioned – The Royal Medical Psychological Association (now known as the Royal College of Psychiatrists) of whose Psychotherapy Section I became chairman. All this, combined with the editing, gave me too little time for developing my ideas on the self in enough detail to make them more comprehensible. I was reproached by Baynes and others that my writing was too compressed and that I had too many ideas on apparently different topics so that my position could not be identified. There was some justification for what was said, in that I tend to write out of myself and without sufficient regard for my audience.

Meanwhile the conflicts with the Society rumbled away and gradually escalated as time went on. My own position in them was partly ambivalent, but on one issue I had been consistently clear and I had expressed it, as I have indicated, when the Society was initiated. I insisted on it being called the Society of Analytical Psychology and not the C.G. Jung Institute. I even let it be known that I would not function as chairman nor help in building up the structure of the body, if the cult of Jung's personality was not firmly resisted. I was and am still much too much of a scientist to support a personality cult. It was on that ground that I contributed to the Society's development. There was, however, more to it than that, for it raised the question of personal and group identity. My understanding of Jung's position was linked up with his idea of individuation, in which each person established his own identity in society. He considered that too much organization stood in the way of individuation and that was why he did not form an Institute in Zurich – it was formed by his students. As an expression of his position he once remarked about the term 'Jungian': 'There is only one Jungian and that is me!' He said nothing explicit about group identity as far as I am aware. This was a problem which was to arise within our Society.

The first sign of serious conflict within the Society arose in 1956 when Simon Stein became chairman. He was an innovative, thoughtful man with a sense of drama, which made the celebration of Jung's birthday in London a delightful occasion. At Jung's celebration dinner in Zurich he conceived the idea of presenting Jung with the cricket ball, suitably inscribed, which had been used in the cricket match we had held against a team of psychoanalysts – we had won. It was a most felicitous gift and Jung put it on his desk. Stein also wanted the Articles and Memoranda changed so that I could be elected president and still take an active part in the

Society's deliberations. I suspect that caused offence amongst the Zurich-orientated members, though I don't known for certain. Finally, he was often not tactful and was given to fits of contempt for inferior work. Whatever the complex of reasons, when it came to his second year of office, Erna Rosenbaum, Gerhard Adler and his wife Hella, with Culver Barker in support, erupted with a demand that Stein stand down. Of course he would not. However, he was not re-elected. I am still ashamed that I did not support him more effectively. Another move, however, was firmly rejected: it was proposed by the Zurich group that the Professional Commit-tee – in effect the training committee – should become an oligarchy and that the four Zurich members should be permanent members of it so as to give them a permanent majority.

The conflict now moved into the Professional Committee, as it was then: that is, without the Zurich analysts having the majority they sought. The committee opposed the closed vessel doctrine: some members of it, and I was one, began to consider carefully what aspects of a candidate's personality we expected to have been analysed and this led on to asking for full reports from the training analyst. That was an indigestible morsel and eventually Hella Adler refused to give any information whatever. So we held some interviews with candidates in order to assess what had and what had not been 'analysed' (I use quotation marks because it was becoming increasingly clear that there were differences in what the term meant). These interviews showed up some alarming features: one candidate had no idea how to elicit a homosexual transference, another became offended when her patient showed signs of a negative transference. This investigation made me, but not others, feel that the Zurich analysts had acquired a quite unjustified prestige, and I was not at all sorry when they showed signs of such serious discontent that they might leave and form a new training on their own.

But many members of the Society were upset and began to question their right to call themselves Jungian analysts. There was a crisis of identity. In their distress I was once more called upon to be chairman of the Society – I had long since ceased to hold that office. I agreed because of their need, but unwillingly, for I had hoped that the members would have formed a viable unit capable of negotiating such crises. A chairman usually held the office for two and sometimes three years, so I stipulated that I would hold it only for one year. I did that with the idea that it would compel Society members to continue with the labour of forming their own identity. I did not want the Society to become a Fordhamian school.

There was not much I could do as chairman other than to be a figure-head who appreciated the acuteness of the conflicts but yet was sufficiently detached from them. I believe I judged correctly and I mostly sat there during meetings – a spectator of the turmoil. During the year there was only one statement that I remember. It came from Culver Barker, a man of great integrity but no genius; he simply stated: 'Back to first principles'. The trouble was that nobody wanted to involve themselves in such a fundamental discussion, which might easily have become excessively intellectual and done nothing to resolve the emotions that were the main problem. Eventually the Zurich analysts (Culver Barker, Gerhard and Hella Adler, Erna Rosenbaum, and Vera von der Heydt) formed their own 'Alternative Training' though retaining their membership of the SAP. I was sorry but relieved, because I considered the group were in serious danger of forming a Jungian creed which Jung himself would have abhorred.

The question of differing trainings had been broached before when I was chairman in the early years. I succeeded in making an agreement with the Zurich Institute that we would both recognize each other's trainings. This involved free access to each other's meetings and lectures. The agreement stands but has not been used. I believe that if Zurich had been less arrogant the SAP, whose responding arrogance was less entrenched, would have been willing to enter into a dialectic about what the other establishment was doing. The Zurich inflation was not to be punctured. They had followed us in forming a training institute and had even introduced, but very inadequately, some clinical matter into it.

It was before the Zurich analysts retired that the Society decided to publish a Journal; then the conflict with Meier took place about whether it should be edited by a committee representing international Jungian societies, and about whether it should be called the 'British' Journal. It is of interest to study what happened. Meier had attributed omnipotent powers to me and so, as he believed I could make the English analysts do what I wanted, a committee view was simply my view. Therefore the demise of his proposition was due to me. This incident promotes reflections on how I led, if that is the right word for what I did: I listened to what our members were thinking and if there was an idea that I liked I would give it my support. On occasion I did initiate projects, but on this occasion the idea grew up in the Society first and that is how it usually was. To a certain extent I was recognized as 'father' of the Society but it was kept so that I never became the omnipotent leader in Meier's sense. That accorded with my intentions. Of course, when the Society fell into disarray, there was not much worth listening to except the disorder, which needed a containing figure-head watching the members struggling to reach a solution.

My relationship with Meier became strained for a time, but was soon sufficiently mended for him to confide in me that Jung had attempted to obstruct his becoming professor at the Eidgenossische Technische Hochschule in Zurich, where he had been teaching for several years. Meier was very hurt and miserable about it and I was able in some measure to ease his pain. Freddie was a good friend and Frieda and I went on excursions with him and his wife to especially good restaurants. On another occasion he took us up mountain roads, which was terrifying – the roads were of a single track and twisted and turned round sharp bends so that if we met a car coming in the other direction both would have been catapulted into space, or at least that was what I imagined would happen.

Once again the Society was in the forefront of developments in analytical psychology: we had started the first training and now we were publishing the first journal. That did not make us more popular, especially since it would be clinically orientated and case material was to be published. And I was in the thick of it. It was at this time that I realized more forcibly the disadvantages of being thought of as a leader. It was assumed, usually outside the SAP I am glad to say, that I could make the members do what I wanted. That was far from the truth. I had my ideas about how the Society should develop but what happened was a collaborative effort all along. My leadership consisted, as I have said, much more in listening to what members said and fostering those trends which I thought desirable.

In the case of discussions which I thought undesirable, I would play off one side against the other in the hope that the discussion would plough itself into the sand of futility.

I have taken an example of a conflict between our Society members and Meier's view, which represented a widespread one outside the Society; but there were tendencies within it that I was not happy about. This was the habit of picking out bits of Jung and bits of psychoanalysis and putting them together without paying sufficient attention to whether they did or did not fit. Murray Jackson's incorporation of Hanna Segal's differentiation between symbolic equation and true symbol formation ran counter to Jung's distinction between symbol and sign; nor did he mention that Jung held that most of the psychoanalytic understanding of the symbol was a form of sign language. That notation was important and almost universally accepted by his followers. In my view the procedure of putting together bits of divergent disciplines is the fault of eclecticism and was an important factor in the Society's identity crisis.

Something like this reproach has been made against me on the grounds that I had done just that myself with regard to psychoanalysis. I had picked up a bit – it was really a large chunk – of psychoanalysis and inserted it where it did not fit. It is true that I had found Melanie Klein's discoveries profoundly important, including her practice of making deep interpretations early on, but that was taken to mean that I was no longer a Jungian and was influencing the Society in my direction. I think that was true, but I never made a closer contact with Klein and never, until old age, did I go for supervision to any trained Kleinian; nor did I ever consider having a Kleinian analysis, because I did not feel the need for more analysis other than my self analysis, and because of my loyalty to Jung and the SAP. None the less, I needed the knowledge which psychoanalysts had accumulated, owing to insufficient work having been done on childhood by Jungians – a defect that I was attempting to rectify.

However, many Jungians felt that what I thought of, and acknowledged, as necessary criticism of Jungian thought and practices was destructive of Jungian theories and practices. For my part I discovered that by critical estimation I could define a field of study to which I could devote myself. I endeavoured to make use of the theories and insights of analytical psychologists as a basis from which to start. So, as Jung thought that the archetypes, but not the fantasies to which they gave rise, were inherited, it would strengthen his hypothesis if manifestations of the archetypes could be found in children – I found them. The other supposedly heretical idea I developed was that the self was active in childhood. That differed radically from current Jungian thinking but I did not develop the concept for lack of supporting evidence. It was, therefore, with some surprise that Jolande Jacobi announced that Jung, in his later years, expressed the view that individuation was a lifetime process, continuing from birth to the grave. He did so without reference to my studies; I do not know how to estimate Jung's view, for which he had very little, if any, evidence of his own.

I did not find the evidence I was looking for until I learned of the mother-infant observations being conducted at the Tavistock Clinic. I asked Martha Harris, head of the Child Psychotherapy Unit at the Tavistock, to depute somebody from her staff who would conduct seminars for our child analysis trainees at the SAP; she lent us Gianna Henry, who had an interest in Jungian thought and practice. It was quite clear from these seminars, which I attended, that mother and infant were two interacting persons. I am deeply grateful to Gianna and the students in these seminars, who produced and interpreted such splendid material.

17   AGEING

The ageing process began when we still lived at St Katherine's Precinct. It was more evident with Frieda, who suffered a number of painful and distressing illnesses. At first they did not interfere completely with her practice nor did they interfere with my work. It all began with Frieda contracting corneal ulcers, which eventually required corneal grafts. They helped greatly but not as much as we hoped since there was retinal degeneration as well, so that in the end she became blind. Although the ulcers did not prevent her working and there were periods when they healed, they were painful and there was a long and distressing downhill path. She also suffered from two strokes, one very slight, indeed hardly noticeable; a second one struck the left side of her body and diminished the use of her left arm and leg. She could, however, still walk and use her arm; indeed she made a considerable recovery, but then she fell down the stairs, fracturing her right arm – the fracture did not heal and the surgeons would not operate because of her osteoporosis. They feared making the condition worse, though the nerves to the limb had become involved in the fracture, rendering the arm virtually useless. Finally she started to become confused and lost real contact with what was going on around her, although she would surprise us from time to time with her perceptive intelligence. Eventually she could no longer use the good book cassettes that the Society for the Blind provided. She could, right to the end, I am glad to say, appreciate the devotion she aroused in myself; in Tony, her son, and her many friends; and the help of May Fowler, a warm, generous woman, who was invaluable. She started as a cleaner but helped in many other ways and became almost part of the family. Towards the end nurses also came in as the functioning of her body and mind gradually disintegrated. She was amazingly courageous and undemanding – not indeed that one could do very much except look after her and be, for as long as possible, a companion. She died in 1987 aged 83, after over ten years of gradual decline.

It was while we were still in London, and Frieda was relatively well, that I had contacted Martha Harris at the Tavistock Clinic asking her if she could 'lend' us a member of her staff to lead the students taking our training in child analysis, for mother-infant observation studies. As I mentioned, she lent us one of her colleagues, Gianna Henry, who had previous experience of Jungian methods both in London and Zurich. It was about this time, in the late seventies, that our lease of St Katherine's Precinct ended and Frieda wanted to retire and live in the country. I was not ready to do that, although I was beginning to feel my age. My mind was still active and I had interests I wanted to follow up so it was arranged that I live with Max and his family during the week and come down to the Severalls, my father's house in Jordans, at the weekends. I found a somewhat dingy consulting room in Hampstead where I saw patients, supervised trainee analysts and conducted seminars on infancy and early childhood. It gave me much pleasure to develop a closer relation with Max, his wife Thalia and my three grandchildren, two of whom I used to take to school on my way to work.

I had hoped that my rather theoretical seminars on childhood would help to orientate the students in the mother-infant observations and seminars, and I looked forward to their bringing material illustrating or correcting what I was teaching. To my distress nothing of the sort happened and eventually I asked Gianna if I could attend her seminars so that I could correlate my theory with the students' work and her management of it. She agreed and I continued for about two years. It was an intensely moving experience and seemed to demolish many of the theories about infancy – of primary identity, the infant lacking boundaries, the development of images and thought in an infant – in fact, much of what I had written in *Children as Individuals* (1969) about mothers and their babies seemed useless. At that time I had relied on the work of others and tried to weave my ideas into them. Gradually I came to realize that I was listening to the students' accounts, which almost demonstrated my own speculations. They asserted that a baby was not only an individual but also integrated, who came into relation with his mother by a process I described as deintegration. The observations appeared to embody a previously abstract proposition: integration and deintegration. But that was not all – I found the impact of the observations a powerful emotional event leading to more difficulties: I fell violently in love with a younger woman.

I was determined that this love would not interfere with my love for Frieda but the conflict was altogether too much for me. I tried talking to Frieda about my feelings – that was a mistake because, understandably, Frieda became alarmed and feared I would abandon her. She could not understand I never would do so. Eros is, however, a mighty daemon and eventually I became ill, gaining the impression that the doctors did not know what was wrong with me. It was clear that I had a virus infection giving rise to herpes of the fifth cranial nerve but it was more than that, and I consulted Dr Bayliss in London, who said the main trouble was my heart and I should go into hospital at once, which I did. But the puzzle remained. I heard a rumour (since denied) that the physician who was looking after me in hospital said that I would either die or if I recovered I would become a cripple. That was not surprising to me as I already thought I was dying. There was about a week when I had no consciousness except for a sense of drifting away and a knowledge that it was an experience of death – very agreeable, I thought.

Eventually I returned to life as follows: there was an assistant nurse who had been deputed to try to persuade me to eat when I would not. One day I heard her say something like, 'I am fed up with trying to feed you, just you eat it up'. This was a revelation: so that is what that stuff in front of me was for! I started eating again and gradually recovered, with the help of the same assistant nurse who also made me walk and would not stand any nonsense. I think permission to drink champagne, in spite of sister's disapproval, was the other main help to recovery – I do not wish to devalue Frieda's devotion nor the generosity of many friends who came to see me but only to emphasize the very primitive levels of experience in which I found myself.

Returning home was very good and I soon decided that I had to do something about my conflicts. I was in no condition to continue my practice in London and decided to try doing so at Jordans, on a much reduced scale, when I was well enough. In the meantime I went to see a psychoanalyst who refused to do anything, but there was Donald Meltzer in Oxford, who would. So I went for what seemed to me once-a-week analysis on the couch. He would not have it that he was analysing me, calling it supervision instead. Whatever it was to be called, I soon felt great benefit and, indeed, I attribute my surprisingly good recovery to his treatment of me. I do not think I could have gone through all the emotional turmoil of my loving two women, let alone Frieda's increasing debility, without my weekly visits to him, nor would I have developed such a rich professional and literary existence. How did it come about that at my advanced age – I think I was seventy-nine when I started with Meltzer – I could at last submit to the ministrations of a Kleinian?

It would have been difficult to go to a member of the SAP; furthermore I had the idea that my pain would be better treated by Kleinian knowledge. In addition I would be getting personal experience of a discipline to which I already owed much and for which I had great respect (of this I have made acknowledgment elsewhere – briefly, I thought that Klein and Jung were investigating the same material from what Bion calls 'different vertices'). I did not mean, however, to become a Kleinian psychoanalyst even if that had been possible, which it was not. Whatever other factors came into it all, the result was admirable and I have not needed to continue regular contact with Meltzer up to the time of writing this book. As I said, it was his suggestion that I should write an autobiography, which started me off on a project that has been therapeutic and has helped me to accommodate myself to growing old. I never thought it would grow into a book that could be published – I thought I might circulate it privately amongst my friends but no more than that.

Growing old is, of course, a gradual process but it was speeded up by my illness. Up to a point a recovery took place, but when it was partly completed I found that all physical acts were slowed down. My mind still worked quite well except for decision-making, which became harder, and a tendency to know what wanted doing and then not doing it. Memory, never my strong point, became worse and was irritating. Hearing worsened and I have had to use a hearing aid after a long resistance. I also developed a tremor in my hands which made writing difficult and, when using a typewriter or word processor, the result is more mistakes than would otherwise have occurred. Those are the main disadvantages I have experienced in ageing.

On the other hand, there is the great advantage of having time to think at leisure which my active life had not provided time for. This has, I believe, made me a better analyst and has resulted in a pulling together of my ideas. Hopefully I have made them more digestible to others by writing, lecturing and giving seminars. I continue to teach the trainees in child analysis, to whom I introduce the essentials of Freud's case material, comparing it with Jung and Melanie Klein. They are willing to come down to Jordans once a week for as long as a year. I was surprised at the number of lectures that I was still invited to give, whilst visitors still came from the States, a few from Italy and elsewhere, some of whom wanted what amounted to periods of supervision covering the technique of analysis and the study of the child in the adult.

One discovery that has come with being ill and growing old has been the number of good friends that I have; I don't mean that my tendency to be guarded about friendship has entirely disappeared, but I have become more open and thankful for friends' personal kindness, generosity and appreciation of my work. An indication arose when the SAP wanted to celebrate my eightieth birthday; one idea was to hold a grand party, but to this I demurred and said I would prefer a number of the Journal devoted to my researches and so it was. Another event came as a complete and very enjoyable surprise: a group of analysts came down to the Severalls, bringing a delicious lunch. They were few enough to talk with each of them and Frieda and I sat in state and enjoyed their generosity. I felt that I was too old to enjoy a grand occasion, as had been arranged on my seventy-fifth birthday, but nothing could have been better than this spontaneous and genuine event.

I now come to the effects of Frieda's debility. I was glad to do what I did: nursing her, feeding her and finding ways of conversing with her, often about the behaviour of her body and mind. She appreciated my using my analytic knowledge about infancy for when she was in one of her periodic 'death trips', as we called them, it would help her revive. Sometimes May Fowler would comment on Frieda's ups and downs and so I had confirmation of my efforts. Occasionally I became bad-tempered and she would relapse. It was during this period that I learned how alarmed she had been about my falling in love. It was also then that she said she regretted part of her will, but she was too debilitated to do anything about it and I had no heart to press her on that subject. We had talked over our wills many years back and I expected that she would not have changed anything important. I was mistaken. Frieda's will was a shock, for she left her half of the Severalls to trustees. She had every legal right to do that but it violated the spirit in which I had given her half-ownership of the Severalls when it was left to me and my brother by my father.

In spite of my wish to look after her as much as I did, and I do not regret doing so, there is no doubt that it meant identifying with her and becoming more depressed than I wanted to recognize, so her sudden death was not the shock it might have been; I was even glad that her GP's effort to revive her did not succeed. That relief was not, I am glad to say, as egoistic as it may sound for I was sure that she had had enough and wanted to die. I worked out a cremation service with the generous help of Lawrence Brown, an analyst and cleric; Stephen Rhys, my nephew and professor of music; and my grandson Cato, who sang with tears in his voice – I was amazed at the power of his voice, not having heard him sing for some time. It was a satisfying occasion, giving opportunity for our grief without the Christian beliefs which neither I nor Frieda could subscribe to. Later there was a burial service in the Quaker graveyard in Jordans. Tony wanted to carry the ashes to the grave, where I placed them and said a few words that I had prepared. A

Quaker then quoted a suitable passage and Max filled the grave with more earth: it was a profound and moving experience in which Quaker simplicity made room for a real spiritual experience.

Although Frieda's death was by far the most important, there have been other losses; my brother died when I was seventy and then there was Jung. Among other valued colleagues whom I miss are Rickman, Winnicott, Simon Stein, and Dennis Newton. Joe Wheelwright miraculously survives, I am glad to say. Mourning is a strange business with all the clash of love and hate, of disillusion-ment and the growth of reality. This refers especially to Frieda, who has become more real as a person. Although I had a long period of thinking I had no future and only had to await death, this did not accord with my many activities: seeing patients, taking seminars, responding to requests for articles in books and journals and writing these reminiscences, not to mention seeing and visiting friends. But at first it was all against the background of death. Gradually, change has taken place and I have come to feel more like a child reaching out into the new life of ageing.

INDEX

Note: MF is used as an abbreviation for Michael Fordham

Adler, Gerhard 93, 95, 97, 104, 110, 130, 134, 135
Adler, Hella 134, 135
Adrian, Lord 50-1
analysis, child *see* child guidance clinics; childhood and infancy
analysis, MF's: with Godwin Baynes vi, 29, 62, 63, 66-7, 69-70, 71-3, 74, 75, 113; with Hilde Kirsch 29, 72, 73-4, 113; with Donald Meltzer 142
Analytical Psychology Club (London) 62, 64, 75, 77, 92-3, 129
Analytical Psychology Club (New York) 65, 122
archetypes 106, 127; children's dreams and 64-5, 117, 122; Jung on 60, 61, 65, 79, 112, 117, 118, 119, 138; and sand tray method 84, 119
Astor, James viii
Auden, W.H. 41, 122

Bailey, Miss 119
Balint, Michael 99
Barker, Culver 93, 95, 134, 135
Barret, Jack 96, 103, 107, 108, 121
Bateson, Gregory 123
Batty, Mr Trevor 20, 28
Bayliss, Dr 141
Baynes, Godwin 77, 78, 91, 133; analyses MF vi, 29, 62, 63, 66-7, 69-70, 71-3, 74, 75, 113; Max Fordham as baby and 63; *Mythology of the Soul* (1940), MF's case material published in 71, 72-3, 74, 130; sings with MF's mother 26
Bedales preparatory school 31, 32, 33
Bennet, E.A. 100, 127
Berkeley, George 48
Berryfield Cottage (childhood home) 28-9
Bertine, Eleanor 122
Bethlem Hospital 56
Bion, Dr Wilfred 79, 100, 142
Bollingen Foundation (New York) 96, 102, 106, 107, 108, 121

Bone, Muirhead, and family 27-8, 29
Bowes Lyon, Miss Lillian 42
British Journal of Medical Psychology, MF writes on autism in 102
British Psychological Society Medical Section 99-100, 132
Broomfield (Alderley Edge, Cheshire – maternal grandparents' home) 7-9, 11-12, 31
Brown, Lawrence 144
Bud (headmaster) 33, 34, 36, 40

Cahen, Roland 107
Cambridge University: Chris Fordham goes to 38; Max Fordham goes to 90; MF reads medicine at Trinity College 46-51; Mr Fordham goes to 21-2
Carmichael, Dr 59
Centre for Analytical Psychology *see* Society of Analytical Psychology
Chandler, Dr Raymond 53, 55
Chesterfield Child Guidance Clinic 83, 84
Childers, Erskine 48
Childers, Ruth 48, 77
child guidance clinics: Chesterfield 83, 84; London 62, 63-4, 65-6, 74, 82, 95; MF criticizes team method 95, 101; Nottingham 81, 83; Sheffield 83-4; University College Hospital 95; West End Hospital for Nervous Diseases 100-1
childhood and infancy, analytic study of: Jung on 63-5, 66, 88, 117, 119, 123, 132, 138; Klein on 65-6, 137, 143; MF on 74, 82-3, 88-9, 101-2, 117, 119, 130, 131, 132-3, 137-8, 140-1; Society of Analytical Psychology training 130, 138, 140-1, 143; in USA 65, 122-3, 125
Children as Individuals (MF 1969) 141
Churchill, Dr Stella 45
closed vessel doctrine 128, 134
collective unconscious 60, 69, 98, 112, 126
Commonwealth Foundation 62, 82

deintegration 101-2, 141
'development and status of Jung's
    researches, The' (MF) 99-100
dreams, archetypal 61, 79; in children
    64-5, 117, 122
dreams and MF's analysis 69, 71, 73, 118
du Maurier, Miss (probably Daphne) 42

Eccles, J.R. (headmaster) 39, 40, 41, 47
Edie, Aunt 11-13, 24
editing by MF 39; *Journal of Analytical
    Psychology* 106-9; Jung's *Collected
    Works* 96-7, 102, 103-6, 109-10,
    113, 115, 119, 121, 122, 132
education: Cambridge University 46-51;
    Greshams school 36-7, 38, 40-1,
    45, 46, 48; nursery school 25;
    patchy academic record 39, 40, 47;
    preparatory schools 31-2, 33-4, 36
Emsworth House (preparatory school)
    33-4, 36
Eranos conferences (Switzerland) 96-7,
    116

Fabian Society conferences 22
fairy tales 64, 65, 129
Featherstonehaw, Miss (teacher) 25
Fiertz, Professor 105-6
Figlio, Karl viii
Fisher, Mrs Corbett 53
Flower, Desmond 62
Fordham, Cato (grandson) 144
Fordham, Christopher (brother) 4;
    career 45; as a child 6, 7, 16, 23,
    25, 28, 31, 32; death 145; goes to
    Cambridge 38; inherits property
    45, 144; suggests MF be a doctor 46
Fordham, Ernest (uncle) 1, 2-3, 4-6
Fordham, Frieda (*formerly* Hoyle -
    second wife) 4, 12, 17, 29, 92, 120,
    125, 141; assists MF with *The Life
    of Childhood* 82-3; burglar hits
    115; death 140, 144-5; founder
    member of Society of Analytical
    Psychology 93; illness and debility
    139-40, 142, 144; lectures at
    Zurich Institute 130; marries MF
    89; Max Fordham and 90, 145;
    owns caravan 99; as psychiatric
    social worker 75, 77, 81, 88, 89;

    visits Jung with MF 113, 115, 117,
    119
Fordham, Sir George (uncle) 2, 3, 4, 5,
    21, 80
Fordham, Herbert (cousin) 5
Fordham, Kathleen (cousin) 5-6
Fordham, Margery (cousin) 5
Fordham, Max (son) 75, 77, 145;
    babyhood problem 62-3; birth 59;
    goes to Cambridge 90; goes to
    Dartington Hall school 90; meets
    Jung 117-18; stays with uncle in
    Jamaica 89-90; wife and children
    140, 144
Fordham, Molly (*née* Swabey - first wife)
    4, 55, 57, 58; birth of Max and
    motherhood 59, 62-3; as journalist
    53, 63, 66, 74, 75; marriage to MF
    53, 66-7, 72, 74-5, 77; presumed
    drowned 89; works at *Vogue* 63, 74
Fordham, Montague (father) 18, 20-3,
    26, 33, 40, 44-5, 109; death 18, 44,
    119; devotion to agriculture 20, 21,
    22, 23, 42, 44; and Dr Stella
    Churchill 45; extends Hillcroft 30;
    family background 1-6, 11, 21;
    goes to Cambridge 21-2; goes to
    White Russia 42; house at Jordans
    53, 140, 142, 143, 144; joins Red
    Cross 34-5; MF associates Jung
    with 67, 69, 79, 111, 112, 113, 115,
    119; *Mother Earth* 22; *The
    Rebuilding of Rural England* 44;
    reliability in a crisis 21, 23, 36, 49;
    remarries 42; *Short History of
    British Agriculture* 20
Fordham, Sarah (*née* Worthington -
    mother) 15-18, 23, 28, 32, 35, 37;
    asthma and poor health 17, 22, 24,
    38; beauty 15, 17, 38; death and
    effect on MF 17, 38-9, 46, 89, 125;
    family background 7-13; MF's love
    for 15, 48, 77; MF with at Clapham
    Junction vi, 27, 29; singing and
    love of music 2, 11, 12, 16, 18, 21,
    26
Fordham, Sydney and Alice (uncle and
    aunt) 3, 5, 22, 38-9
Fordham, Thalia (daughter-in-law) 140
Fordham, Thea (sister): as a child 6, 7,

16, 18, 25, 28, 31, 32; Home
   Student at Oxford 38,
Fordham, Thea (cont.), literary interests
   and friends 42, 44; plays lacrosse
   38; in 'secret service' 35
Fordham family 1-6, 11, 21, 31
Fowler, May 140, 144
Foy, Mr (biology master) 40
Franklin, Cecil 45
Franklin, Dr (paediatrician) 63
Franz, Marie Louise von 104, 115, 129
Freud, S. 60, 71, 83, 98, 112, 143
Frey, Toni 129

Galsworthy, John (godfather) 22-3, 42
Garnett, David 25, 42
Garnett, Edward and Constance 22, 25-6
Gee (preparatory school matron) 33
German Society for Psychotherapy see
   International General Medical
   Society for Psychotherapy
Gilmore, Jean 121
Glover, Alan 104-5, 109
Greshams school 36-7, 38, 40-1, 45,
   46, 48
Guild of Pastoral Psychology 117, 132

Hampstead, childhood home in 38-45
Hannah, Barbara 96, 113, 129
Harding, Esther 122, 129, 131; Journey
   into Self 126; Psychic Energy 125;
   Woman's Mysteries 125
Harris (paediatrician) 82
Harris, Martha 138, 140
Hawkey, Lawrey 65, 81
Head, Henry 44
Heimann, Paula 129
Henderson, Joseph 75, 94, 108, 126
Henry, Gianna 138, 140
Heydt, Vera von der 130, 135
Hicking, Mrs (psychiatric social worker)
   85
Hillcroft (Steep Hants - childhood home)
   15, 30-8
Hoffer, Dr Willie 98
Hope, Sister 56-8
Hopkins, Gowland 50, 51
Howell, Dr Hinds 53, 54, 55, 59
Hoyle, Frieda see Fordham, Frieda
Hoyle, Pat (stepson) 89
Hoyle, Tony (stepson) 89, 140, 144

Hull, Richard 96, 97, 102, 104, 106,
   109-10
Huxley, Julian 27, 29, 40

illness: after mother's death 39; nursed
   by Sister Hope 57; serious and
   recovery from 141-2, 143
infantile autism 64, 101-2
Institute of Medical Psychology see
   Tavistock Clinic
International Association for Analytical
   Psychology 99, 131
International General Medical Society for
   Psychotherapy 77, 79-80, 97-8, 99

Jackson, Murray: on symbolism 131, 137
Jacobi, Jolande 103, 108, 113, 122, 129,
   138
Jacobi, Mario 129
Jordans (Bucks), father's house at 53,
   140, 142, 143, 144
Journal of Analytical Psychology 132,
   135, 136, 143; MF edits 106-9
Joyce, James 44; Ulysses 47, 48
Julia 66
Jung, C.G. vi, vii, 71, 73, 100, 108,
   110-20, 125, 127-8, 136, 143;
   advises MF on change of analyst 72,
   113; alleged anti-Semitism 67, 79,
   97-9, 111-12; Answer to Job 120;
   on archetypes 60, 61, 65, 79, 112,
   117, 118, 119, 138; astrological
   experiment 105-6; on child
   analysis 63-5, 66, 88, 117, 119,
   123, 132, 138; Collected Works
   (co-edited by MF) 96-7, 102,
   103-6, 108, 109-10, 113, 115,
   119, 121, 122, 132; on collective
   unconscious 60, 69, 98, 112; death
   (1960) 111, 119-20, 145; deplores
   religiosity 117, 132; Emma Jung's
   work and 115; Essays on
   Contemporary Events 99;
   extramarital affair compared by
   Baynes with MF's 67, 72; on
   individuation 133, 138; informality
   and formality 72, 113, 115, 119;
   Memories, Dreams, Reflections 65;

Jung, C.G. (cont.), MF connects with Klein 29, 66, 142; MF first meets 67, 69, 111–13; MF sees comparison between his father and 67, 69, 79, 111, 112, 113, 115, 119; MF's last visit to 119–20; MF visits with Frieda Fordham 113, 115, 117, 119; MF writes for 70th birthday 99–100, 103, 117; on myths 66, 93, 130; on need for medical training 75, 93–4; as only 'Jungian' 133; outspokenness 115–17; at Oxford conference of International General Medical Society for Psychotherapy 77, 79–80; personality cult 94–5, 133, 135; presented with cricket ball 133; *Psychological Types* 106; *Psychology and Alchemy* 97, 102, 104, 106; psychology of types 75, 79, 106, 127; *Psychology of the Unconscious* 66; on psychosis 61, 70; Rorschach test and 124; on sign and symbol 131, 137; on synchronicity 105; Tavistock lectures 77, 78–9, 103, 113; on transference 78–9, 118, 128, 130; visits England 72, 77, 78–80, 113

Jung, Emma 113, 119; interest in child analysis 64, 77, 117, 119; lay analyst 94; study of Grail symbolism 115

Jungian Institute (San Francisco) 75

Kalff, Dora 64, 119
Kirsch, Hilde: analyses MF 29, 72, 73–4, 113; in USA 74, 124, 125
Kirsch, James 73–4, 113; in USA 74, 108, 124, 126
Klein, Melanie 65–6, 83, 137, 143; MF connects with Jung 29, 66, 142; *The Psychoanalysis of Children* 65
Klopfer, Bruno 124–5, 126
Kretschmer, Professor Ernest 97

Lambert, Kenneth 132
Langley Porter Clinic (San Francisco) 123
Laszlo, Violet de 125
lay analysts 93, 94
Letty, Aunt 12
Lewis, Aubrey 109

Life of Childhood, The (MF 1944) 82–3, 88, 131
Limpsfield (Surrey), childhood home at 24–6
London Child Guidance Clinic 62, 63–4, 65–6, 74, 82, 95
London School of Analytical Psychology 131
Long Grove Mental Hospital (Epsom) 58, 59–62
Los Angeles, visit to 124–5, 126
Lowden, Miss (social worker) 64
Lowenfeld, Dr Margaret: sand tray method 64, 84, 119
Lucas, John 108

Maberley, Alan 54, 60, 62
Mace, A.C. 109
McGuire, Bill 106, 109, 121–2
marriages: to Frieda Hoyle 89; to Molly Swabey 53, 66–7, 72, 74–5, 77
Maw, Miss 85, 86–7
Mead, R.G.S. 12–13
medical qualification, analytic training and need for 93–4, 127
medicine: degree at Cambridge 46–51; general practice 58, 70–1; at St Bartholomew's Hospital 52–8
Meier, C.A. (Freddie) 80, 98, 99–100, 108, 113, 129; disagreement with 107, 135–6, 137
Mellon, Paul and Mary 96
Meltzer, Donald viii, 142
Meredith, Carew 47–8, 54
Metman, Phillip 93
Moodie, William 82, 95
Moody, Robert 93, 128–9
mother–infant observations 138, 140–1
mythology 60, 61, 66, 93, 130

nanny 25
National Hospital for Nervous Diseases 55
National Institute for the Blind: Sunshine Homes 82
Navy, ambition to join vi, 32–3, 36
Neumann, Eric 108
neurology vi, 54–5, 59
New Developments in Analytical Psychology (MF 1957) 106, 118, 128, 131

Newth, Dr 81
Newton, Dennis 100, 145
New York: Analytical Psychology Club
    65, 122; visit to 65, 106, 121–2,
    123, 125, 126
'Notes on the transference' (MF) 118,
    128
Nottingham 81–90, 91, 92; Child
    Guidance Clinic 81, 83; evacuee
    children 85–9
nursery school 25

Objective Psyche, The (MF 1958) 131–2
Odsey (Herts), Fordham family property
    in 1, 2–3, 5, 6, 21, 45

paintings 64; by children in evacuee
    hostel 85–6; by MF in analysis 71,
    73
Paulsen, Lotte 93
Phillips, Porter 55–6
Plaut, Fred 4, 129
Posthuma, Dr 82; 'passive technique' 63
preparatory schools 31–2, 33–4, 36
psychiatric social worker(s) 85, 94, 123,
    127; Frieda Fordham as 75, 77, 81,
    88, 89
psychiatry 82, 95; at Long Grove Mental
    Hospital 58, 59–62; see also child
    guidance clinics
psychoanalysis 55–6; MF's first attempts
    at 60–1; MF's view of Kleinian
    theory 29, 65–6, 137, 142; Society
    of Analytical Psychology and 129,
    131, 137
psychoanalysts 69, 123, 128, 142; in
    British Psychological Society 99;
    cricket match against 133; criticize
    Jung 97, 98, 112
psychotic patients 56, 60–1, 70–1, 87

Ramsey (Cambridge Fellow) 48
Read, Herbert 96, 97, 103, 104, 110, 116
Rees, J.R. 97, 99
'Reflections on the archetypes and
    synchronicity' (MF) 106
'Reflections on individual and collective
    psychology' (MF) 100
religiosity and analytical psychology 117,
    132
Rhees, Mrs Jean 82

Rhys, Ernest, and family 37
Rhys, Stephen (nephew) 144
Rickman, John 99, 100, 145
Rosenbaum, Erna 91, 93, 95, 134, 135
Royal College of Physicians Membership
    examination 53–4, 58
Royal College of Psychiatrists (formerly
    Royal Medical Psychological
    Association) 55, 132
Russell, Bertrand 48

St Bartholomew's Hospital vi, 59, 75;
    Jung speaks at Abernethian Society
    77, 113; MF house physician at
    53–8; Schuter scholarship 52–3;
    Strauss offers posts at 83, 95; war
    prevents child guidance post at 82
St Katherine's Precinct, house in 139,
    140; burglar 115–16; flying bomb
    lands 92
San Francisco: Jungian Institute 75; visit
    to 122–3, 124, 125, 126
Santa Barbara, visit to 123–4
Scharf, Riwkah 129
Schmidt, Miss (Jung's secretary) 103–4
Scott, Clifford 99
Seddon, James 108
Segal, Hanna 131, 137
Self and Autism, The (MF 1976) 101, 102
self theory in infancy and childhood
    88–9, 101–2, 132–3, 138
Severalls (Jordans – father's house) 53,
    140, 142, 143, 144
Sharp, Cecil 18
Sheffield Child Guidance Clinic 83–4
Society of Analytical Psychology (SAP)
    83, 92–3, 100, 127–38; conflicts in
    93, 131, 133–5, 136; identity crisis
    129, 134–5, 137; Journal 106–9,
    132, 135, 136, 143; MF rejects C.G
    Jung Institute as name 94–5, 133;
    training of analysts 91, 93–4,
    127–31, 134, 135, 136, 140–1,
    143; Zurich analysts and 95, 128,
    129, 130–1, 134, 135
Society of Jungian Analysts of Southern
    California 124
Stanford University (San Francisco) 123
Stein, Gertrude 44
Stein, Simon 107, 133–4, 145
Strachey, James 96

Strauss, Eric 83, 95
Swabey, Molly *see* Fordham, Molly
symbolism 131, 137
synchronicity 105, 106
syntonic countertransference 128–9

Tavistock Clinic: Jung lectures at 77, 78–9, 103, 113; MF trains at 77–8, 94; mother–infant observations 138, 140–1
Thomas, Edward 31
Tor Gardens, One (Campden Hill London – MF's birthplace) 22, 24
Toynbee, Arnold 108–9
Trail, Miss (therapist) 84
transference 83, 112, 113; in children 66; ignored in MF's analysis 66, 71, 72, 74; Jung on 78–9, 118, 128, 130; MF's interest in 66, 74, 84, 118–19, 128–9, 132; in psychotic patients 60–1

United States visit and lectures 121–6; Los Angeles 124–5, 126; Mexican border 124; New York 65, 106, 121–2, 123, 125, 126; San Francisco 122–3, 124, 125, 126; Santa Barbara 123–4
University of California at Los Angeles (UCLA) 124–5
University College Hospital, post offered at 95

vocation, analysts and 93, 94, 126
Volkovski, Vera (*later* Fordham-stepmother) 42

Walk, Dr (psychiatrist) 61
Wasserstein, Dr (translator) 104
Watts, Harvard 108
Welch, Mrs Marged and Mr 91, 93
Well Walk, Forty (Hampstead – childhood home) 38–45, 53
West End Hospital for Nervous Diseases: Child Guidance Clinic 100–1
Wheelwright, Jane 123, 124
Wheelwright, Joseph 73, 75, 94, 122–3, 124, 126, 145
Whitaker, J. Ryland: anatomy course in Edinburgh 50; *Anatomy of the Nervous System* 50
White, Victor 132
Williams, Gianna viii
Winnicott, Donald 145
Wittgenstein, L. *Tractatus* 48
Wolff, Antonia 79, 94
Worthington, Claude (uncle) 7, 34
Worthington, Edie (aunt) 11–13, 24
Worthington, Hubert (uncle) 7, 8, 9, 11, 12
Worthington, Letty (aunt) 12
Worthington, Mrs (grandfather's second wife) 7, 8–9, 11–12, 34
Worthington, Percy (uncle) 11, 12
Worthington, Thomas (maternal grandfather) 7, 8–9, 11–12, 18
Worthington, Tom (uncle) 7
Worthington family (mother's family) 7–13, 31, 34

Zurich Institute 29, 129–30, 133, 135
Zurich-trained analysts 95, 118, 128, 129, 130–1, 134, 135

This first edition of
The Making of an Analyst: A Memoir
was finished in November 1993

The book was commissioned by Robert M. Young,
edited by Karl Figlio,
copy-edited by Julia Henderson,
proofread by Ruth Levitt,
indexed by Linda English,
and produced by Ann Scott and Chase Production Services
for Free Association Books